TEN POWERFUL PHRASES

for Positive People

RICH DeVOS

CENTER
STREET®

NEW YORK   BOSTON   NASHVILLE

Center Street
Hachette Book Group
237 Park Avenue
New York, NY 10017

Visit our Web site at www.centerstreet.com.
Center Street is a division of Hachette Book Group, Inc.
The Center Street name and logo are
trademarks of Hachette Book Group, Inc.
Printed in the United States of America
First Edition: November 2008
10   9   8   7   6   5

Library of Congress Cataloging-in-Publication Data
DeVos, Richard M.
Ten powerful phrases for positive people / by Rich DeVos. — 1st ed.
        p.   cm.
Summary: "Amway cofounder Rich DeVos inspires and motivates business leaders
with simple but life-changing practical lessons rooted in his real-life experiences."
—Provided by the publisher.
ISBN-13: 978-1-59995-098-3
ISBN-10: 1-59995-098-7
1. Success.   2. Oral communciation.   3. Interpersonal communication.
4. Relationship quality.   5. Psycholinguistics.   I. Title.

BJ1611.2.D48 2008
158—dc22

                                                    2008012197

This book is dedicated to Billy Zeoli.

Contents

CONTENTS

Preface

When I celebrated my eightieth birthday in 2006, I described the velocity of my years as "zero to eighty in ten seconds." Eighty years sounds like a long time until they're behind you. But it's not really how fast time goes that matters but how wisely we use the precious time that God has given us.

After eight decades, I can reflect on the whirlwind of activity and thank God for blessing my life far beyond what some would simply describe as luck. I look back on a few, but very important, gifts that have been constants in my life, and I'm amazed at how they're all connected in His plan.

I was raised in a home that was short on material things but long on love. I grew up in an encouraging atmosphere that taught me nothing is more valuable than love for one another and a strong faith in God. I had the benefit of a Christian home and a Christian church and school. My wife, Helen, and I have been married for more than fifty years, have raised four children, and have been blessed with their spouses and sixteen grandchildren. I've never taken for granted the gift of a loving family and try never to miss opportunities to tell my wife, children, and grandchildren how much they mean to me.

Another constant in my life has been maintaining a positive attitude and affirming others. The value of using simple phrases to be positive and helping others be positive was crystallized for me by a very dear friend of mine, Billy Zeoli. I was well aware of the power of phrases, but he presented them in an especially clear and dynamic way. I decided that rather than just adopt them casually, I would use the phrases by design.

The purpose of this book is to help you, too, keep positive phrases top of mind and in your vocabulary, to help you be a "life enricher"—someone who encourages other people in his life.

The late Dr. D. James Kennedy of the Coral Ridge Presbyterian Church in Fort Lauderdale, Florida, used to say to me, "You are the most positive person I have ever known." I was thankful for that, because that's what I was trying to be. And he was well aware that I appreciated him and was encouraging him to keep doing his best and recognizing him for the good job he was doing. Now, that's really not difficult. It's something all of us can do when we make a decision to be a positive person. From the time I gave my very first speech, I was determined to talk about the wonderful things about our society and our world instead of looking for things that were wrong. I wanted to enrich the lives of those in my audiences and beyond.

So I've been using the phrases that Billy emphasized for me and adding a few of my own, just as I hope you will. My real hope is that they will help you become a positive person who, in turn, will help other people improve their outlook on life. And if we all do so, I truly believe we can make a real change for good in our homes, communities, and world.

Thank you for picking up this book. I'm encouraged by your interest in being a positive person. Learn these phrases and use them daily with the people who mean the most to you. Some may be difficult to say, but practice them and you will be rewarded by the results. I truly believe that we all have the power to contribute to a more positive society and world. Best wishes as you carry this out.

Richard M. DeVos

Acknowledgments

While I hope this book is an acknowledgment of the many individuals who have had a positive impact on my life, I wish to offer special thanks to: Helen, my wife and ever-present positive partner who also was a very skilled editor on this project; my children and their spouses—Dick and Betsy, Dan and Pam, Bob and Cheri, and Doug and Maria—for their enduring support; Marc Longstreet, who helped me convey my thoughts in the pages of this book; and, Kim Bruyn, for her persistence in encouraging me to write this book and for guiding it from start to finish.

Introduction:

The Art of Being Positive

I was honored to receive a 2007 Norman Vincent Peale Award for Positive Thinking. When my lifelong friend and business partner, Jay Van Andel, and I started selling Nutrilite vitamins in the late 1940s, one of the first books I read was Peale's *The Power of Positive Thinking*. We also had Dr. Peale speak at some of our Nutrilite sales conventions, and I got to know him well.

Peale was a shy student who was encouraged by a college professor to believe in himself and believe that God would help him. He prayed and believed and became the founder of the concept of positive thinking. He once said that his happiness was the main reason he was so concerned about people who are not happy. He was bothered that unhappy people were not using all their creativity and that society was suffering for it. He decided he wanted to do something about it and shared his ideas in speeches and books.

The Norman Vincent Peale Award for Positive Thinking is given each year to recognize people "whose lives clearly and inspirationally exemplify the power of thinking positively, with faith, deep caring for people, and dedicated commitment to improving our world." I don't know if I've lived up to that glowing description, but those words match my goals in writing this book.

I've by and large been a positive person ever since I can remember. I was happy as a child despite growing up during the Great Depression. I've tried all my life to inspire others to use their talents and fulfill their potential. As cofounder of Amway Corp., I've delivered motivational messages to thousands of people around the world whom I wanted to see achieve their dreams in their own Amway businesses. I'm a cheerleader to my players on the Orlando Magic NBA franchise and a community leader in helping rally my hometown of Grand Rapids, Michigan, to keep building and growing.

I've learned that positive thinking and encouragement are essential for leadership and progress. As the leader of a company or your own children, you'll find that positive thinking is infectious and a concentrated fuel for change.

I was raised by a father who remained positive, even after losing his job during the Great Depression, and who always encouraged me. Jay Van Andel and I had no other ambition than to build a business of our own, and we remained true to that goal despite a list of setbacks. We once rented a hall that seated two hundred for a presentation to recruit distributors for our nutritional products. Only two people showed up! But we stayed positive and built a business we could never have imagined. People would congratulate us on all we had built. However, we didn't spend much time looking back on what we had accomplished. We were too busy thinking about what we could do next.

Although people seem to need to vent and grumble at times, they are drawn to the positive and will follow those who blaze a positive trail. I've addressed arena-sized audiences, but one of my first speeches was to a group of forty accountants. One of my employees in the early days of our Amway business had invited me to speak. I started thinking about what I would say and just began jotting down all the positive things that had been happening in the early growth of our business.

So many other speakers I'd heard seemed to want to prove their intelligence by telling the audience what was wrong with the world. That was their claim to fame and credentials. They found something for which they could be an "expert critic." I told my audience of accountants that I wasn't going to be a critic; I was going to tell them about the good things going on in this country.

After that speech, I presented my positive message to other groups. The more I spoke, the more people responded. At a time in our history when people were beginning to doubt democracy and see socialism as the future, I pointed out all the positives we enjoyed as free American citizens. Once I started on that theme, people began giving me additional information to use in the speech. One day someone handed me a list of comparisons between the standard of living in the United States and the communist Soviet Union that clearly demonstrated why we had so many reasons for being positive instead of negative. So I began to use it, and those examples became a powerful tool to remind Americans how blessed we are. I discovered that people in my audiences appreciated being reminded of how and why they could get into the habit of looking for good in their lives and in other people.

That little message I first delivered to a few accountants

grew into "Selling America," a speech I eventually delivered to thousands across the country—and which later was recorded and received the Alexander Hamilton Award for Economic Education from the Freedoms Foundation. I discovered that the more I talked about being positive, the more people wanted to hear.

Maybe they were hungry for positive news, because the world is full of negative communicators. Just read the letters to the editor in any newspaper. Finding fault is easy and a natural instinct. Maybe it's because we're taught to be skeptical. We know that if it sounds too good to be true, it probably is.

My hope for this book is that I can encourage people to seek the positive. That can require a little energy and some retraining, but anyone who makes the effort will reap great rewards in helping themselves and others. A positive attitude is a choice, like walking to the other side of a street to avoid trouble or making a 180-degree turn when you feel you're headed in the wrong direction.

Once we decide to make that choice, being positive becomes a habit. When we meet someone, for example, we listen to find something good about what they are doing, because sooner or later they will tell us. If you stay tuned you will always hear good things, because everybody wants to do a little bragging. So if we express interest and listen, we'll get clues about the good things they are trying to do. Then we can respond with a positive phrase that fits: "You can do it!" "Thank you!" "I'm so proud of you!" The words simply flow out of you after a while.

A positive frame of mind changes you and how you think, enabling you to lift up other people. You begin to seek goodness, and therefore, you begin to feel better about everything, including yourself and the positive things you're doing. All of this self-esteem comes from simply developing the habit of looking for good in others. When that happens, you begin to see the good in yourself as well, and then people begin to recognize that good in you and praise you for it. It becomes self-fulfilling.

When I graduated from high school, my Bible teacher wrote a line in my yearbook that I never forgot—just one simple line of encouragement: "To a clean-cut young man with talents for leadership in God's Kingdom." His line was simple but a great source of encouragement to me as a young man, as one who was not a good student and had been told he was not college material. But a teacher whom I admired saw me as a leader! Wow! I'd never thought of myself in that way before.

The point is that a simple line can change a person's life. So the question is, what kinds of lines are you delivering? What kinds of lines have you heard? Are you going to create a negative atmosphere or an encouraging atmosphere for people? Are you going to drag them down or lift them up? I decided to be a life enricher, to find a way to lift people up. It's as easy as expressing a simple, yet powerful phrase: "I'm proud of you." "I need you." "I believe in you." "I love you." Those can be world-changing lines for some people. They should be in your vocabulary.

The principles in this book are for everybody, but they apply in a special way for people who aspire to leadership positions. Making the first move to be positive is a trait of great leaders. Whether you lead a company, play a leadership role as a teacher or coach, or are a leader as a parent or grandparent, these powerful phrases will help you.

Consider leaders who were effective because they were positive. The U.S. presidents you remember are the ones who had to deal with tough situations and made them look pretty good. Franklin Roosevelt's fireside chats during the darkest hours of World War II were not negative stories. Ronald Reagan was a storyteller par excellence. He dealt with tough issues. But he always had a funny story. He always left you laughing. He always found the good side of an issue. John Kennedy knew he had to have a positive mission for our nation, so he said, "Let's go to the moon!" He challenged America with a dream to move up, go beyond, and do better. The nation adopted this goal, and fulfilled it in 1969.

Those in leadership positions need most of all to develop these traits, to learn these phrases, to practice the art of being positive. Leadership is one of our great shortages. We need people who will stand up and get the job done, whatever that job may be. Leaders have the power to be examples for the rest of us to follow.

I also know from experience that people can work together to create a positive atmosphere in their community. Positive people in my hometown of Grand Rapids have helped lead amazing progress in recent years. A few years ago, I was speaking to a dinner crowd at the opening of our convention center. I reminded them that we lived in the right climate. They were probably taken aback, because it was snowing and freezing that evening. But I wasn't referring to the weather. I was talking about a climate of positive people who work together to keep improving their community. Together, we had built this marvelous convention center: Community leaders instilled the vision, government and donors provided the dollars, tradespeople supplied the skilled labor, even those whose smaller role might be overlooked—a very capable wait staff all talented in their own way—efficiently delivered a delicious hot meal to each of the twenty-five hundred guests.

Even beyond our own communities, citizens with a positive attitude could have the same impact on our nation and even our world. If everybody in this country started to have a positive attitude, started looking for the good and began to compliment each other rather than complaining and finding fault, it would cause a dramatic social change—one in which we would all lift up each other. We would work harder, think better, come up with more ideas, dream bigger, make greater contributions, and feel better about ourselves and our world. Our country and society suffer when we cannot find the good in anyone or anything. Our Congress and president must have *some* good ideas and be doing *something* right. But the politicians on both sides of the aisle seem to find it hard to bring themselves to say so. When we avoid debate or constructive criticism and instead pin derogatory labels on each other, we are developing a culture unable to use positive phrases.

I love the verses in Philippians 4:7–9 (NIV): "Whatever is true, whatever is noble, whatever is right, whatever is pure, whatever is lovely, whatever is admirable—if anything is excellent or praiseworthy—think about such things." Think what our world would be like if everyone took those words to heart! That's why I wanted to write this book and why I think a positive message is so important in today's world.

I thought a simple way to encourage a positive attitude would be to offer some of these Powerful Phrases for Positive People. Nothing profound or earth-shattering, but that's the beauty of it. These ordinary, unassuming little words contain hidden power that, when released, can change lives for the better in profound ways. But this book goes far beyond the phrases. Our decision to live with a positive attitude can change us, our community, and even our entire nation and world. I truly believe it's time for a revival in our country. We need a shift in attitude toward positive thinking and positive actions that can heal relationships and bind us together for a common good.

Like those inspiring U.S. presidents and all great leaders, you too can improve conditions when you lift people up and inspire them to do more. I firmly believe the message in this book is of vital importance to our society today. Every society needs people who can encourage and stimulate and cheer. They are the ones who make the world run. You can be one of them!

1

"I'm wrong"

I chose to begin with "I'm wrong," because it's the hardest of the phrases to say and genuinely mean. It's tough to admit when we're wrong, even to ourselves, and harder still to say out loud, "I'm wrong" — especially to those whom we care for most or want most to care about us. I learned that lesson many years ago when my wife, Helen, was scheduled for cataract surgery. The doctor said she could arrive in the morning and go home the same day of her surgery. That sounded fine to me. But Helen said, "No, I don't want to rush in. I want to go in the night before. I want to be there, relax and be cared for, and I don't want to have to get up and hurry in the morning before I have my eye surgery."

Thinking only of my own inconvenience, I mumbled and grumbled about the extra time and the cost of her being in there overnight. But Helen went in the night before, and the next day the doctor said it would be okay for me to scrub and watch the

3

operation. I was able to observe through a magnifying device as the surgeon delicately extracted the old lens and created a framework for the new, artificial lens. Watching this intricate process I suddenly realized what a big deal this was. The need for Helen to be rested and emotionally relaxed struck me. I was thinking only of the convenience of getting in and out as quickly as possible. After her surgery, I apologized to Helen; I told her I was wrong and she was right. I've had to do that a lot of times, too, because she's a really bright lady, and I've been known to be wrong a few other times in my life. But at least I'm learning that if we are more sensitive to the views of others in the first place, we are less likely to put ourselves in situations where we'd have to say we were wrong.

Saying "I'm wrong" is meaningless unless it comes from our heart, not just our lips. That often requires a genuine and profound change within ourselves, because we need to accept that we can be wrong. Even if that admission hurts, we need to realize it's simply human nature and that everyone makes mistakes. We also need to realize that we can have a positive impact on the lives of others when we admit to them that we were wrong.

Our outward expression of admitting wrong can serve as an example of our willingness to change and can inspire others to change in positive ways. A positive impact stems from our admission that we were wrong or our thinking was wrong. "I'm wrong" are two little words that can help improve our own positive attitude. It's all part of this shift in our decision to create a positive atmosphere instead of a negative one. If you've been wrong, say so!

I'm afraid it's becoming too easy to come up with examples of organizations that create negative atmospheres because no one is willing to say, "You know, I may have been wrong about that. You're absolutely right!" How would that go over in a union negotiation or during a debate in Congress or at the dinner table after a family argument? I know from experience that such an admission would take a lot of negative air out of the balloon.

Admitting you're wrong is especially difficult for people in leadership positions. The leader is supposed to be the visionary, the bright one who covers all the angles and blazes the trail for those better equipped for following than leading. Unfortunately, even leaders at times have to admit they're wrong. I had to be shocked into that reality as the cofounder of my company. I would propose a new method or introduce a new product, confident that I'd looked at every possible angle. Someone would ask, "Did you think about this? Or that?" "Oh, sure, sure. Of course," would be my initial response. But thinking back, the fact might have been that I really had *not* thought about it. I had missed it completely! Someone with a different point of view had noticed something that I myself hadn't thought about at all.

This type of situation poses a choice: Preserve your pride by covering yourself and not admitting your oversight, or simply say, "You're right! I'm wrong! Somehow I missed that." The ability to admit you were wrong allows you to correct mistakes and work together toward solutions. Admitting you are wrong creates opportunities to learn from mistakes and to take advantage of another person's point of view. I had not shown respect to my employees by seeking their opinions.

Because I chose to admit I was wrong, I learned the value of getting my employees' perspectives and discovered the importance of holding regular meetings in the early days of our Amway business. We called these meetings "Speak Up." Every few months we would select a representative from each department to meet with me. They were free to ask any questions, submit suggestions, or even complain about anything, from something as big as a glitch in the system to something as small as the food in the vending machines.

"Speak Up" was a way of letting our employees know that we didn't have all the answers, that we were capable of mistakes, and that we respected their opinions. We acted on employee suggestions from those sessions to build a better company. In doing this, I set myself up for the possibility of having to admit I was wrong to my employees. It was one of the smartest business decisions we ever made.

Our stubborn will to be right all the time can drive a wedge between friends or family members. At times the urge to be right can lead to arguments that aren't worth winning and in hindsight are just plain silly. Jay Van Andel and I maintained a friendship and business partnership for more than fifty years. We could not have achieved that rare accomplishment without reaching agreement on all our important goals and business decisions. Because Jay was older, he served as chairman and I as president on a board of two. We agreed both of our votes were needed to approve business decisions.

In the early days of our Amway business I was driven by ego to want a bigger car. Distributors we had sponsored were driving Cadillacs, and Jay and I were still driving Plymouths and Desotos. A car dealer in downtown Grand Rapids had a beautiful, elegant Packard that I very much wanted to own. I bought it as a company car without asking Jay. I had to apologize for that one. He passed it off. He said, "That's okay, you made a decision; you enjoy it." I got my way, but I violated our own corporate policy of both of us agreeing on capital expenditures.

So what huge business decisions did we ever find to argue about? Believe it or not, it was deciding the dress code for the restaurant on the top floor of our new Amway Grand Plaza Hotel when it first opened in the early 1980s. One of the most insignificant decisions in our partnership led to one of our biggest disagreements.

Cygnus, twenty-six stories above downtown Grand Rapids in the tower of our new hotel, was the first elegant restaurant in the city. The debate was whether we should maintain a formal restaurant with a dress code including jackets and ties for men or be less restrictive and open to more diners and perhaps more business. That was the only time in our long partnership that one of us had used the veto word. Fortunately, we had a strong friendship, and the Cygnus decision could fade into a triviality. But friendships and even family relationships have eroded or ended over even more trivial arguments. For most people, having to admit you're wrong dents your pride and your ego. It's one of the most difficult things most people will ever have to say.

But it does get easier as we grow older, when, one hopes, we have more achievements than mistakes and are not so delicate and easily threatened. With age, you've made your share of mistakes in life and have admitted to yourself and others that you're far from perfect. When we're young and trying to establish ourselves, we fear admitting a mistake. The reality is admitting mistakes is liberating for ourselves and others and is a mark of maturity. Our admission is a sign of strength—that we can be humble and aren't too big to admit when we're wrong. People appreciate humility. Nobody likes a know-it-all.

Saying "I'm wrong" is also the beginning of a healing process. The first inclination of the child caught with a hand in the cookie jar is to deny, defend, rationalize, and make excuses. Just like the child, our first inclination is to furiously defend our position rather than admit to someone or ourselves that we are wrong. Denial and rationalization are hard and fruitless work. We grow only when we place greater importance on healing a relationship than defending our position. Understanding that everyone errs in life takes the sting out of being wrong. Admitting we are wrong is the only way to truly heal the hurt we may have caused others. Without it, people tend to bear a grudge and develop wounds that may never fully heal.

Wrongs are inevitable, and denying their existence only creates arrogance and strife. We are not perfect, nor are we intended to be. Perfectionists face the need to be perfect in all they do. Who could ever live up to such standards? Laugh at a wrong—laugh at yourself! Your ego will only take you so

9

far, but your integrity and humility will carry you through to success.

Acknowledging our wrongs may even heal us physically as well as mentally. Medical science continues to find ever greater connections between our physical and mental health. I'm not a doctor, but I believe it's obvious that admitting guilt rather than working hard to defend, forgiving instead of carrying a grudge, and accepting ourselves—faults and all—can reduce a lot of angst and hand-wringing that can damage our physical health. We most likely will feel better both mentally and physically when we release ourselves from the burden of always having to be right and the fear of others who might judge us for being wrong. So I've tried to become enthusiastic when I say I'm wrong. I'm not quiet about it. I'll openly acknowledge when someone is right and I'm wrong. And it's just as important to tell others that they were right as it is to say that I was wrong.

We all need to know that despite our mistakes, most people can find it in their hearts to forgive and eventually even forget. We can also return the grace by forgiving others when they have been wrong. One of the best examples I can think of is the character of Gerald R. Ford. I lost a friend and the nation a revered leader when President Gerald Ford passed away the day after Christmas in 2006. Jerry Ford grew up in my hometown of

Grand Rapids, Michigan, was a star on the national championship University of Michigan football team, and was our U.S.
congressman for many years. I was thrilled and proud when my
friend and neighbor became president of the United States and
greatly saddened at his funeral service and burial in my city.

The news coverage following his death was a testament to
him as a humble man who proclaimed his reliance on God's
leading during his presidency. His integrity and faith were never
more apparent than when he pardoned Richard Nixon. President Ford knew this pardon would likely jeopardize his 1976
presidential campaign, but he did what he believed was right.
In a speech to the nation explaining the pardon, Mr. Ford said
he could not expect God to show him justice and mercy if he
was unable to show justice and mercy to others. He looked beyond politics and personal gain to forgive and forget in the interest of healing our nation. As President Ford realized before
most Americans, the future of the country mattered much more
than the fate of a former president.

We waste energy when we hate someone rather than forgive him. Jesus told us to forgive our enemies. We also need to
forgive ourselves, knowing God can forgive us for any sin we
confess. I can picture President Ford in the Oval Office, des-
perate to heal our nation, eager to move our country forward,

and reaching the conclusion that his only choice as a Christian and leader was to put the past behind us through a pardon and look ahead. We can make the same choice. A positive future is more important than any grudge we might hold against another person, or any guilt we might harbor from past mistakes.

Frequently when I speak, I introduce myself with these simple words: "I'm just a sinner saved by grace." This started nearly twenty years ago when I was asked to address a group of serious-minded Detroit businesspeople getting together in a swank hotel to hear about business success from me. Most members of the audience knew little about me other than my business achievements. The emcee gave me a long, flattering introduction about my success in helping build an international corporation and cited some of my awards, board chairmanships, and honorary doctorate degrees. It seemed to go on forever. When I finally got to the podium, I thanked him for the generous introduction but explained to the audience that they should know who I really am—"just a sinner saved by grace." The line just came out, and it stuck. I've often introduced myself with those words since then because I view my faith as my life's most important asset.

When I was growing up in Michigan, winter typically meant heavy snowfalls. I remember when falling snow would nearly blot out the street lights and drift over the roads. We awoke on winter mornings to a world covered in a fresh layer of brilliant white powder. A pure, freshly fallen snow can make us appreciate why the psalmist used snow as the measure when asking God to forgive his sins and wash him white again. It's hard to imagine anything whiter than a new blanket of snow glistening in the morning sun. Yet we have the promise that the saving grace of God can wash us whiter than snow. No matter what we might have done in the past that we regret, of which we are ashamed, or that we wish we could take back, God can wash away without a trace.

"I'm wrong" is a powerful phrase for positive people because it can wash away the pain of a strained relationship, move a negotiation forward, end an argument, start a healing process, and even turn enemies into friends. It can be a risk for most people. Admitting you're wrong can be a threat to your authority and credibility and stature, but most things worth having in life require some risk.

Throughout my career I've used my sailing experiences as examples of risk-taking, making the point that you'll never learn to sail by standing on the shore. I've often told the story of how Jay and I sold our early business ventures shortly after World War II and bought an old wooden sailboat. We set out from

Connecticut and headed down the coast toward our planned destination of South America—despite the fact that neither of us had ever sailed a boat. We got lost, we went aground, and once were so off course the Coast Guard had trouble finding us. Our leaky boat eventually sank off the coast of Cuba, but we continued our travel by other means to South America and learned a valuable lesson about taking risks and moving forward with confidence. If you wait until you have all the knowledge and experience you think you need, you'll never take a risk or achieve a goal.

During the time that Amway Corp. took a huge risk by expanding with our first overseas affiliate in Australia, I delivered a speech to our independent distributors called "The Four Winds." My message was that the four winds come from all points of the compass; some days they blow with you, and some days they blow against you. Our success depends on how we cope with different winds. In those days I was sailing on Lake Michigan a lot. The west winds could be gentle, and I'd sail along with the breeze. On rare days the wind would switch to the east, and I knew I was in for unusual and unpredictable weather. When a northwester comes across Lake Michigan on the heels of a cold front after humid weather, the lake starts to boil, and you need to know how to handle your boat or get out of the race.

For me, whatever the wind blows my way, hope is constant. When you're out on the water, the wind blows a lot of unsettling conditions your way. So does life. And those unsettling conditions — those changes in our circumstances — can break us or make us. It's not how we handle the good days that determines how well we do in life. It's how we handle the bad days. In a sailboat in unsettling conditions the sailor can adjust the sails. In those unsettling moments when we are wrong, we need to adjust our thinking by accepting our mistake and considering how we can best settle things with the other person. Summoning the courage to say "I'm wrong" is how we cope with difficult situations. It takes risk but pays huge dividends, and you'll never know until you say the words, "I'm wrong."

I can no longer imagine jeopardizing my relationships with my family or friends because I'm afraid or too stubborn or threatened to say, "I'm wrong. You were right. I'm sorry and please forgive me." Life is too short. An ego is neither too large nor too fragile for a person to heal a wound and repair a relationship with a few simple words.

"I'm wrong" shifts our attitudes and opens us to the benefits of healthy relationships as we look for ways to be positive. It's hard to be wrong and harder still to admit to someone when you're wrong. But we all need to learn that hard lesson. Do you know in your heart you've been wrong but never truly admitted it to yourself or someone who should know? What would happen if you said to that person, "I'm wrong. You were right." Try it. You'll find it's not as daunting as you might imagine, and it will keep getting easier.

2

"I'm sorry"

Along with saying "I'm wrong," we have to be sorry for it. By being wrong we may have hurt somebody in the process, so our admission must be more than something technical or mechanical — simply saying the other person was right, and we were wrong. When we wrong someone, that person is going to respond to us and spill some anger. We have to let him or her know we are sincerely sorry for what we did. It's so easy to try to defend our position, but it's amazing how many problems disappear once we decide to say we're sorry. All the anger and emotion fall away. The positive impact far outweighs our reluctance to admit we have feet of clay or to risk a loss of stature and bruises to the ego.

My youngest son, Doug, had heard several times as a teenager a speech I had been giving on the topic of powerful phrases, including the power of using "I'm wrong, and I'm sorry" to end any argument. As I pointed out in this speech: "The beauty of saying 'I'm wrong, and I'm sorry' is that it quickly ends an argument. Once someone admits to being in the wrong and apologizes, what's left to say?" One night when Doug missed his curfew I was waiting up for him. The later the hour, the more perturbed I became. I was really going to lay into him as soon as he came through the door. The door finally opened, and Doug crept into the house and saw me waiting for him. He knew he was late and saw that I was angry. But he made no excuses. He quickly and simply announced to me, "Dad, I'm wrong, and I'm sorry." I had been fuming, but after Doug admitted he was wrong and said he was sorry, what more was there for me to say? Besides, I think he even sincerely meant it — at least at that moment!

"I'm wrong" and "I'm sorry" are companions. They're really healing words for your apologies. "I'm sorry" is a tag for "I'm wrong," but it's also separate. And like "I'm wrong," it's a phrase that has to be learned and is difficult to say.

A lot of our political leaders and celebrities would do well to learn this lesson. When was the last time you heard a public apology — an "I'm sorry" — from well-known figures in response to their indiscretions or mistakes? They are more adept at using words that defend their positions. From presidents and congressmen caught in lies and scandals to rock stars and athletes caught in criminal or socially unacceptable acts, we hear a lot of public relations spin and rationalizations, but a simple "I'm sorry"—unless forced to the wall to save their careers—is rare. The truth is, the American public would likely appreciate their humility, empathize with them, and forgive and soon forget if they voluntarily offered an immediate and heartfelt apology. Two words could avoid a prolonged rash of negative news stories.

Defending positions, using words to cover up rather than to enlighten, blaming the other guy and shirking responsibility can all occur when we choose a negative course instead of making a decision to be positive. This behavior perpetuates a slide toward a negative society. We see this negative trend today among our leaders in Washington, D.C. Our country was founded on moral values. Our leaders reached decisions through thoughtful debate and a commitment to achieving a higher good. Differing opinions were welcomed and respected in order to reach the best solutions. Political parties may have differed in how to achieve goals for the country, but in the end they could agree they were all Americans and that members of either party could conceivably offer ideas worthy of consideration and respect.

From my experience with government, it appears we no

longer welcome debate. Republicans and Democrats want to do it their way or no way. A Democrat cannot find a single compliment for a Republican president. A Republican can find no merit in a Democrat's bill. The truth is, we have ideas of merit on both sides of issues and both sides of the aisle. We must be able to appreciate the other people and their points of view and be willing to compromise to arrive at some positive legislation.

The ability to say "I'm sorry" shows that we are able to see the other person's point of view, that we want to maintain a relationship, and that we are not too big to reach out and see the good in others. An apology is a conscious decision we reach when we have empathy for the feelings of others. Instead of thinking of the apology only from our point of view as an admission of our wrong-doing, we consider how our apology will benefit the person we have wronged and actually have a positive impact on his or her life.

In the late 1980s, I was struck by something Walt Disney had written, and I used his words as the basis of one of my speeches. Disney said there were three types of people: "Well Poisoners," who criticize and try to tear people down rather than build them up; "Lawn Mowers," good people who do their jobs, pay their taxes, and take care of their families and homes but never venture beyond their own yards to help others; and

"Life Enhancers," who by their kind words and deeds enhance the lives of others and leave their world a better place for having lived.

At the end of the speech I read the story of Miss Thompson that was written by Elizabeth Ballard in 1976. You can read the entire story in Charles Swindol's book *Quest For Character,* but in short it's about a schoolteacher and one of her pupils who was unloved and struggling in class because he'd never had a decent home life or anyone to care about him. Seeing his school records and disheveled appearance, Miss Thompson also ignored him until something happened at Christmastime.

While the other students gave Miss Thompson new gifts that their parents had purchased for them, this unlikable, underachieving child gave her a gaudy rhinestone bracelet and some cheap perfume that had been his mother's before she died. The other students started to laugh at his gift. But Miss Thompson had the good sense to stop them by trying on the bracelet, wearing some of the perfume, and commenting favorably about his present. Miss Thompson also prayed that night, asking God to forgive her for ignoring this child that no one seemed able to love and vowing that from that day on she would try to see the good in this once neglected child. They started a friendship that continued through his graduation as a doctor.

On his wedding day, he invited Miss Thompson to sit where his mother would have sat if she were alive.

Like the story of the Good Samaritan, the Miss Thompson story is a reminder of our obligation to lift up others. The Miss Thompson story is unusual only because it is rare. Most people choose to ignore the person in need of being lifted up. We can use our positive attitudes and positive phrases to connect with people. Instead of defending our position and trying to place blame, we can empathize rather than criticize. We can be humble instead of arrogant. That's why the ability to say "I'm sorry" is so important.

There are also a lot of things you can be sorry about that you're not wrong about: "I'm sorry that you have lost a loved one." "I was sorry to hear of your illness." "I'm sorry you failed to land that position for which you worked so hard." Being sorry shows our empathy and humility when we express our condolences for a loss or sympathize with someone's difficulty.

We also can be especially helpful to our children or grandchildren when they face disappointments that are part of growing up. Some of these things may not seem major to us from our adult viewpoint, but they can be very hurtful to young people who are trying to prove themselves and seek approval or avoid embarrassment. There have been times when I've seen a child's mood or demeanor send the message that he or she faced some kind of setback that day. Not every child makes the team or is cast in a starring role. These are the times when we can put our arms around them and say, "I'm sorry. I'm proud of you for trying. Keep trying, because I know you can do it!"

Another form of saying "I'm sorry" is apologizing for being unable to attend a function or grant a request. This is a different aspect of sorry: I'm sorry for something I couldn't do — "I'm so sorry I had to miss your party," or, "I'm really sorry I couldn't join you for dinner last night." We need to say, "I'm sorry I couldn't be there," in a spirit of love and respect.

As a grandparent with a full calendar of my grandchildren's many events, I'm especially aware of when I can't attend one, so I have to say I'm sorry a lot. Each day on my printed schedule is a listing — high on top — of what my grandchildren are doing that day. Even if I can't make an event, I let my grandchildren know with a phone call or card that I am thinking of them, that I am proud of them, and that I'm sorry I cannot be with them. In this way, saying sorry even creates another opportunity to communicate with my grandchildren. But saying "I'm sorry" also means that I'm aware of what they're doing. So when I do miss an event, at least I can let them know that I was with them in spirit and that I was sorry for not attending in person.

We also need to admit to ourselves as well as others when we are sorry for past mistakes or errors in judgment or when we have regrets for failing to seize an opportunity or for doing less than we might have done. I myself am sorry that, when our company was growing, we didn't push harder to promote freedom and free enterprise along with the business. Perhaps other businesspeople are feeling the same way. Not being vigilant about protecting the freedom we've enjoyed as a nation and free enterprise as the basis of our economy is coming back to bite all of us. The United States is slipping toward socialism. I'm feeling sorry, almost guilty, that we weren't more aggressive.

Trying—even if we fail—is better than having to say sorry later. Even if we don't achieve success in a venture, we've had the experience, we've enlarged our thinking, and we still may have achieved more than we'd ever thought possible. Jay and I once owned a restaurant. The restaurant failed, but at least I found out two things: how hard it is to make money running a restaurant, and that it definitely was not a business for me! Everyone should try something like that once and get it over with.

The ability to apologize requires seeing a situation from another person's point of view. That means taking an interest in people—even in those who may be nothing like us. I've been called a people person. Being a people person simply means you like people, try to understand them, show an interest, and try to see things from their point of view. You cannot sincerely say you are sorry or express sympathy without understanding other people and their situations. When I'm in one of our hotels, I like to walk through a kitchen or an area where staff are stationed to say hello and thank them for their work. I like to walk around the Amway Arena and talk to employees before my Orlando Magic team takes the floor. People tell me they're fascinated to see how quickly and easily I can strike up conversations with everyone from a new next-door neighbor to fellow patients in a waiting room.

My grandchildren will never forget the time we were vacationing in the Marquesas Islands near Tahiti, and I befriended a man who lived in a hut on the beach. He had a big smile that showed only two teeth. He knew the island well, so I hired him to be our guide to a remote waterfall. That waterfall turned out to be one of the most beautiful spots on the island, a place we never could have explored without his help. We never would have enjoyed an experience like that had I not made a move to get to know a stranger.

That's why "I'm sorry" is a healing touch. The words let the other person know you understand and truly want to make amends or offer support. We've all been there: Working up the courage to say "I'm sorry" after an argument in which we know we were wrong; entering a funeral home and trying to find the right words to say to a friend who's just lost a loved one; having to reassure a friend whose confidence has just been shattered by a rejection letter.

Life is filled with events for which the phrase "I'm sorry" can be powerful. Expressing these two little words may be difficult at times, but getting into the habit of using this phrase is well worth the risk and will enrich your life and the lives of others. You will turn from feeling you need to rationalize or defend what you know in your heart was behavior that was wrong or hurtful. Saying the words will lift the burden of a conscience weighed down by keeping silent. Your words will be enriching to the person to whom you apologize. Saying "I'm sorry" will validate your concern for them and your desire to patch a relationship that otherwise might be damaged or ended simply for the failure to say two words.

3

"You can do it"

A student asked me at a college banquet recently, "What's the most important thing a young person like me should know?" And I said to her, "You need to develop a philosophy of 'You can do it.' Whatever you want to do, you can do it." She seemed surprised. Maybe no one had ever told her this before, so I was grateful for the opportunity to try to have a positive influence on a young person.

"You can do it" has been a defining phrase in my life. The best way to share the power of this phrase with you is to share some of my history that was powered by the philosophy of "You can do it." I was fortunate as a young person because "You can do it!" was the positive phrase my father always used to encourage me. It's a line that I've become known for because I went on to use it to help motivate Amway distributors around the world. I've kept that line in my vocabulary to use with my own children, grandchildren, and other people whom I care for and want to see fulfill their potential. "You can do it" has been a slogan in our home, and I believe it's had a positive impact on our children.

When I was growing up, during the Great Depression, the thought that I could do anything during those hard times had to be instilled in me. My family had to leave the house where I'd spent several wonderful years of my boyhood because my father was out of work and could no longer afford to keep it. Our family had to move into the upstairs rooms of my grandparents' house, where I remember sleeping under the rafters. We lived there for about five of the worst years of the Depression. But those weren't bad days for me as a boy. My cousins lived in the neighborhood. There weren't many cars around, so we could play ball in the street. Our ball would get so beat up that we'd have to wrap yarn around it and stick rags inside. We couldn't *afford* a new one.

Money limited us in those days. I started a paper route to earn money and walked that route until I made enough to buy a used bike. Ten cents was a huge amount of money. I remember a man coming to our house selling magazines and crying because he couldn't go home until he sold the last one. My father told him honestly that we didn't have a dime in the house. Yet my father continued to encourage me with, "You can do it."

My father was a very positive man. He believed in the power of positive thinking. And he preached it even though his own life wasn't as successful as he would have hoped. Yet he never turned negative. He would always tell me, "You're going to do great things. You're going to do better than I've ever done. You're going to go further than I've ever gone. You're going to see things I've never seen."

My mother admitted that she was not very positive early on. However, one day after my father died she told me, "I've decided I'm going to have to be positive if you're going to come over to see me, because you aren't going to come over just to listen to me complain." So from the day of her decision she began to be positive. She honored my father's belief and "did it." I was so proud of her! And that was one more affirmation of my belief that being positive is a decision—something we can learn if we focus on looking for what's good in life and in other people. It also shows that if you're a positive person, your attitude will rub off on others, and they'll be less likely to be negative when they're around you.

I was blessed to grow up in a positive atmosphere. Later in

life I paid tribute to the value of a positive atmosphere in one of my speeches called "The Three As: Action, Attitude, and Atmosphere." We all want to take action. But our actions stem from a positive attitude. And a positive attitude is developed when we are in or choose to put ourselves in the right atmosphere. My atmosphere was the love of that close-knit family that found happiness during the depths of the Depression and believed in a better tomorrow. I was fortunate to attend a private school, Grand Rapids Christian High School. My parents worked hard and made sacrifices to send me to that school. I was doing just enough to earn passing grades—much to the disappointment of my father, who then took me out of the school and sent me to a public school to learn a trade as an electrician. I soon realized all I had lost by goofing off. I decided to return to Grand Rapids Christian High School and told my parents that I'd do odd jobs to earn the tuition. The second time around I was more serious and earned better grades. I was even elected president of my senior class.

To this day I'm grateful for earning the privilege of attending a school that reinforced the lessons of faith, optimism, and hard work that I was learning at home. When I decided to return to Grand Rapids Christian High School and offer to pay my own tuition, it was the first time I ever made a decision with consequences. I realized that I would not have been happy as an electrician and that maybe my father's dream for me could be a vision to guide my life. That school was also where the respected teacher I mentioned earlier wrote that simple, but memorable, line in my yearbook that changed my life, "with talents for leadership in God's Kingdom"—another affirmation of "You can do it."

High school also was where I met Jay Van Andel and started a lifelong partnership. Jay's dad owned an auto dealership. So Jay, during those hard times, was one of only two students in our school with a car. I can still picture everyone piling into Jay's car after school—packing the seats, overflowing into the rumble seat and even standing on the running board of his Model A Ford. I paid him twenty-five cents a week for rides to school.

Conversations during those rides were filled with the dreams of youth for a bright future and laid the foundation for our careers as business owners. We were convinced that we could do it. I look back on my remarkable life of starting a number of businesses, raising a family, and living to enjoy my grandchildren as being based on that foundation of "You can do it!"

Jay and I made a pact in high school to own some type of business together. Upon returning from service overseas in World War II, we started a flying school, even though neither of us knew how to fly. We started one of our area's first drive-in restaurants without any restaurant experience. And eventually we started Amway in 1959 from the basements of our homes.

So from this positive atmosphere, I became a positive person. And with my father's encouraging words of "You can do it" ringing in my ears, I felt confident that I could. My wife, Helen, calls me adventurous, citing as an example my taking our family to places around the world where she never would have imagined going. But I'd just say, "Let's go there! Let's try this." I think seeing life as an adventure is a perfect description of the positive "you can do it" person.

I achieved success in business beyond my wildest dreams. The greatest blessings from this experience have been the satisfaction of achievement through using my God-given talents, providing business opportunities to millions, employing thousands who support families, and sharing my success through philanthropy with Helen. Driving over a rise in the countryside near Ada, Michigan, people come upon the view of a complex of manufacturing plants and office buildings stretching for a mile. At the entrance are fifty poles flying the flags of many of the countries where the company has affiliates. This is the Amway world headquarters. People who see this and know the success Amway has achieved credit Jay and me as visionary businessmen who planned our success. Baloney! The truth is, we were just a couple guys trying to make a living and support families like anyone else. We never could have dreamed of one day owning a company with billions of dollars in annual sales, affiliates in scores of nations, thousands of employees, and millions of independent business owners worldwide.

We were blessed to grow up in a positive atmosphere and possess talents that were God's gifts. Our business started building in our hearts and minds with the encouragement of "You can do it," and the confidence instilled by loving, positive parents and teachers.

A "can do" attitude begins with a simple philosophy. My father's phrase was, "You can do it." Back in the early 1970s, I was giving a speech in which I called the decision to be positive, "Try or cry." I've joked that I've often given the same speech but with different titles. Looking back at "Try or cry," I can see that I've been on the same crusade for decades of trying to motivate people to see the benefits of a positive outlook. I told my audiences that you really can put people into two categories: Those who are willing to try, and those who would rather not try and instead sit on the sidelines and cry about their lot in life and criticize those who do try. I told them we were living in an age when it was not only easy to be a critic, it was popular.

I reminded my audience of the laundry list of ventures Jay and I tried, and how we kept trying after failures: our aviation business, drive-in restaurant, importing mahogany products, building wooden rocking horses, selling bomb shelters. The market for flying lessons never peaked after World War II as people had dreamed. We dumped trays of hamburgers that were left too long under the broiler because we weren't professional short-order cooks. For years we had an inventory of springs and wooden wheels left from the toy horses we decided to manufacture—just as a major toy company introduced a beautiful molded-plastic model.

But we kept trying. We knew nothing about chemistry, manufacturing, packaging, engineering, or human resources when we started Amway. Our first experience trying to run a labeling machine left more labels on the walls, floors, and ourselves than on the packages. But we built a company that today employs thousands of people producing thousands of products that are sold by millions of our distributors known as Independent Business Owners.

Today, "You can do it" has become a slogan repeated around the world in the Amway business. In Japan or China and other Asian countries where Amway has affiliates, you can hear distributors cheering and saying "You can do it." They ask me to sign books with "You can do it." It's become a rallying cry in Asia. That positive phrase has carried around the world to people who have often likely been told they cannot do much of anything. When Amway opened in Russia, I was asked to call from my home in Florida and tell a meeting of about six-hundred people "You can do it!" Our people over there told me it was the most raucous meeting they ever had. These Russian people were excited by the idea of being free to have their own businesses and doing something of substance for themselves. I was told people were standing on the chairs, singing and cheering—an atmosphere more like a football game than a sales meeting. The theme of "You can do it" was incredibly powerful to them!

As I mentioned, my children also have grown up with "You can do it" as a theme in their lives. I've always told them they can do whatever they feel they're led and able to do and that we would support them, believe in them, and encourage them.

After I retired, our oldest son, Dick, succeeded me as president of Amway. I got out of the way and let him run the company. Dick led our expansion all over the world because he had a "You can do it" attitude. In fact, he had been head of our international division for several years because he had that "You can do it" attitude. He then started his own business and in 2006

TEN POWERFUL PHRASES FOR POSITIVE PEOPLE

decided to run for governor of Michigan, because he still had that "You can do it" attitude. When he told me of his decision to run, I said, "Boy, it isn't a very good time for that, is it?" I cautioned him that he would be running against an incumbent Democratic governor in a strong Democratic state. He told me he understood that but had no question in his mind about his ability to do the job and was going to run.

On election night, with only 10 percent of the votes counted and Dick behind, we were all trying to be positive when Dick walked into the room. He announced that he had just called the governor and congratulated her on her win. We were all trying to be hopeful but Dick had been realistically studying the numbers and the districts and realized the race was over.

I visited him shortly after the election, and he told me he felt terrific. He said he had the best time running in his campaign, met the nicest people all over the state, and had a really great experience! Even though he lost the election, there was never a question in his mind about whether he could have done the job. The attitude of "I can do it" was obvious in everything he did.

My second-oldest son, Dan, decided to go into business for himself after being an executive at Amway for many years. Leaving the company was a courageous move, but he also had that "You can do it" attitude. Today he is a very successful owner of several businesses. That's further evidence of a "You can do it" mindset.

When the time came for a family member to manage the daily operations of the Orlando Magic, our daughter Cheri and her husband, Bob, both of whom had been interested in sports, offered to move to Orlando for three years and take over the job. They had no experience in this field, but they had no doubt in their minds about their abilities. So they went to Orlando to take over the team and stayed the three years plus eight more! They had the "You can do it" attitude and demonstrated that they could.

When my youngest son, Doug, went to Purdue University, he studied business and management with the plan of one day running Amway—which he now does. Again, that was part of a "can do" mindset. He joined the Purdue football team as a walk-on quarterback—demonstrating the confidence that comes from growing up in a "can do" culture. He jokes that his football career at Purdue consisted of only a couple of plays. But he did it!

As parents, we need to create that positive atmosphere in our homes. We need to encourage our children that they can do anything they set their minds to do, and that God will bless them and keep His hand upon them. We need to teach our children to trust in God and trust in themselves, believing that God gave them great ability and talents to make a difference in this world.

One of my greatest "You can do it" experiences was when I decided ten years ago to tackle the merger of our two largest hospitals in Grand Rapids. There was constant competition between these two hospitals: If one had a neonatal unit, the other had to have one, too, and so on.

One hospital was considering rebuilding on a new site. I was chairman of the other's board, and I said, "You know, before they build, I think I really would like to take a crack at merging these two. They're only three miles apart, so for best serving the community, it just makes sense." Our president told me, "You know it's been tried before." I said I knew that but times change and I wanted to try. So he agreed, becoming that first vital person one always needs for support. And I was sitting there thinking, "If we pull this off, it's really going to be huge. Merging these two hospitals may go down as the biggest thing I've tried, ever!"

I encouraged the two hospital boards to cooperate — not worrying about how many seats each would have on a merged board, or who would be president or chairman. We took one small step after another and gradually got concurrence from more and more people until finally the boards merged. Then the Federal Trade Commission got involved, saying that we were trying to limit competition. They pointed to me as a staunch free enterprise advocate and asked how I could support anything opposed to competition! But I convinced them that publicly owned hospitals are different from private enterprises, and the judge eventually ruled in our favor.

That's an example of a "can do" attitude despite huge challenges. Thanks to the support of both hospital presidents and many other people, both hospitals today are stronger than they were, and each specializes in different critical needs for our community. We created the critical mass of equipment, facilities, and staff to create centers for excellence that has created a "medical mile" in our downtown and a medical community that is our region's largest employer.

"You can do it" also describes the spirit of America and our free enterprise system that has been so important in my life. Helen and I recently contributed to the People's President Gallery at Mount Vernon in the hope that this exhibit will help preserve and restore our nation's respect and gratitude for George Washington and others who won the freedoms we enjoy today. The exhibits are visible reminders of this great leader who played an essential role in winning our freedom and creating our nation. As a young man Washington was a brave horseman who helped tame the wilderness. He grew into a courageous leader fighting against formidable odds in battle and a wise first president who helped invent the United States of America. Of interest to me as a business person, I also learned that he ran six businesses at Mount Vernon.

I discovered that a visit to the Reagan Ranch is an inspiring reflection of President Reagan's American spirit and character of rugged individualism, idealism, and hard work. When I was fortunate to be invited to a White House dinner, I learned that anyone who asked Mr. Reagan about politics received his standard response, "The office is closed." Then he would lighten the atmosphere with a joke. He exuded confidence and optimism, never seeming to be wondering or worrying. He knew he could do it! And one of his favorite phrases, "It's morning in America," demonstrated his outlook.

I was once privileged to be the narrator for a Grand Rapids Symphony performance of *A Lincoln Portrait* by Aaron Copland. If you haven't heard this piece, it blends inspiring music with the words of Abraham Lincoln. He was the epitome of "You can do it." He began life in a dirt-floor, one-room cabin on the empty plains of Indiana, and despite a combined year of formal education in several prairie schoolhouses was elected president of the United States. Before his presidency, he failed as a shopkeeper and was defeated in races for the U.S. Congress and Senate.

It's no surprise that we've had "can do" presidents, because we live in a "You can do it" country. The first settlers who landed in Jamestown and faced the necessity of surviving against incredible odds in the wilderness with winter approaching must have felt they could do it, or they never would have sailed across the Atlantic to come here. Our ancestors fought one of the most formidable military giants in the world, the British army, to win our independence. The framers of our Constitution created a document that has served our nation for more than two hundred years.

We also need to develop a "can do" attitude among all people. We have all dealt with people who obviously don't have a "can do" attitude, who are always negative, always complaining. Being a "can do" person has greater ramifications. We have great opportunities to be positive people who encourage more "can do" people. Our positive attitudes can be vital in protecting a climate of opportunity in which our children and grandchildren can achieve great things.

When we started Amway, we thought, *It's okay to start a*

business to make money, but what's the ultimate purpose of our business? What does it stand for? What's driving it emotionally, beyond just trying to make money? When we thought about owning our own business, we thought the opportunity to do so was fundamental to America. We thought everyone who wanted to should be able to have their own business. From there we made it our cause to stand up for free enterprise.

The world at that time was going down the road to socialism and communism. Fidel Castro had just taken over Cuba. The Soviet Union was expanding in Asia and Africa. Many were saying, "Free enterprise is dead. God is dead." People thought communism was the wave of the future and would even expand into America. Standing for free enterprise was our battle cry. Many times we were ridiculed for that, but we took it on nevertheless.

Finally, the "can dos" took over in America—especially in the Reagan years. As I said, Ronald Reagan was a "can do" guy. And America became a "can do" society. President Reagan recognized that if you reward your "can do" people properly, they will produce more and more, which helps to take care of the "can't do" people by providing jobs. Helping people economically is really a question of what we can do to help create more jobs—and watch the unemployment numbers decline.

We need to encourage and support the person with ambition who takes the risks and is willing to work hard to start the type of small business that creates so many of our jobs today. It's amazing what a little encouragement can do.

I'm a supporter of an organization called Partners Worldwide. The organization partners businesspeople, farmers, and anyone running his or her own enterprise with someone in another country—usually a third-world country. The American partners are mentors to their counterparts in other countries and help them become more successful.

Partners Worldwide also has a small loan department to help a person buy a sewing machine or a bicycle repair machine or a better plow or tractor—any machine that can help them be more efficient. More than half of the people supported by Partners Worldwide have been able to increase their number of employees because of these efficiencies. Partners Worldwide is hoping to find a million mentors. An interesting side note is that these mentors are discovering that they have a calling as businesspeople. Instead of just going to church and sitting in the pew, they now are missionaries. And the people they are helping have the clear message of "You can do it." They are "can do" people who are achieving on their own and hiring other "can do" people.

It's important to encourage a "You can do it" attitude in others and within yourself. Sometimes it is the only thing that drives a person to accomplish his goal. Let me give you an example. The Internal Revenue Service actually has officials assigned full-time to Amway. I used to kid one of the IRS men about the fact that I kept him in a hall instead of giving him an office in his early days at the company. Finally one of my employees said, "You really must give these guys an office." I said, "Why? Let them sit in the hall. I don't want to make them comfortable!" But we eventually did give them an office.

One day I said to the official who had been there for years, "Are you still here?" And he said with a smile, "I'm your partner." Imagine. I'm your partner! That fearless field representative had an unwavering "You can do it" attitude despite his environment. He did his job dutifully. For that, he earned my respect.

You never will discover how far you can go if you don't start "doing it." Otherwise you limit your whole life and will always have regrets, thinking, *I wish I'd tried that*. When you develop that "can do" attitude, it all happens, and the Lord then supplies you and begins to give you answers. You weigh obstacles honestly, but you consider them as just something to overcome instead of a reason to do nothing.

Even if you do it and fail, you have the strength and the courage to know how far you did get so that you're going to try again, or do it differently next time, or take on a new job with greater confidence. Think about what you could do and just take a whack at it. Think big!

Too many people never try to do anything because they're afraid—afraid of failure, that someone might criticize them or laugh at them, that they don't have enough training or expertise. To them I say, "Set a goal and go for it. *You can do it!*"

4

"I believe in you"

Once, at a silent auction, I was the winning bidder for a signed copy of Norman Vincent Peale's book, *The Power of Positive Living.* Glancing through that book reminded me how much his philosophy influenced me when I was just starting out in business.

I was especially struck by the second chapter of *The Power of Positive Living,* "Be A Believer = Be An Achiever." We cannot achieve our highest goals without believing in ourselves. One of the most effective ways we can help others achieve their dreams is to assure them, "I believe in you."

"I believe in you" is a more personal phrase than "You can do it." A belief in someone is really an extension of the phrase of "You can do it." We typically say "I believe in you" to our family and close friends. But we need not always *say* the words. We can demonstrate "I believe in you" through our actions. Sometimes simply our presence at an event or support of a cause says, "I believe in you."

The title of my first book, written more than thirty years ago, was simply *Believe!* The book was a statement of some of the things I believed then and continue to believe today. The philosophy and message in the book was the same one I conveyed in my speeches to audiences across the country. I wanted to help people start believing in themselves and others. I expressed my belief that America is the greatest country in the world, that our free enterprise system is the reason we were the most economically successful nation, and that each person has human dignity and a reason for being. I continue to encourage people to believe, because to me that's key to helping build better communities, stronger families, higher-achieving and happier children, and employees who fulfill their career goals. So I want to do whatever I can to let these people know I believe in them and encourage them to believe in themselves and go on to achieve more than they thought possible.

When you think about it, so many of our institutions really are built on a belief system. We have to believe in one another as married couples and as family members. We need to believe that our employers and government leaders are acting in our best interest. And we need to believe in our democratic way of life and free enterprise system as the best opportunities for living our lives as individuals. We must believe in ourselves and our abilities to care for ourselves and achieve our own goals.

We need to be vigilant in guarding against the influence of those who show by their words or actions that they do not believe in us. We all have a tendency for self-doubt. And that tendency can be reinforced by naysayers. Too many people accomplish little more than a list of regrets because they doubted rather than believed—because they decided to listen to the negative opinions of others rather than try for themselves. These people could have used a powerful boost by hearing the phrase, "I believe in you."

I've tried to do whatever I can to help the Orlando Magic players believe they can be champions even when the standings and opinions of sports reporters might tell them otherwise. With a name like Magic, we should be an example of a team that believes. Years ago, when the team was headed to the playoffs for the first time, I wanted the players to believe that they could win the championship. The Magic had never won a championship, so it would be easy to understand if the players had trouble believing that they could be champions. They were maybe thinking a championship was something other players and teams achieved, but not them. On top of that, the sportswriters and so-called experts were saying they were too young and inexperienced.

One night I addressed them in the locker room and told them to tune out the negatives. I asked them these questions: "Why not us? Why not now?" That became our battle cry for the playoffs. We posted that slogan in the locker room. In fact, I have the slogan on a wall in my home and still look at it for inspiration. The Magic didn't win the NBA Championship that year, but I think I helped the players believe in themselves and let them know that I believed in them.

"Why not us? Why not now?" That sentiment sums up how we should believe that we can achieve. We have to believe that we can be the winner, the achiever, the successful person who reaches goals. We have to start now, because if we keep waiting and wondering, we'll never do anything.

Our children are most in need of hearing "I believe in you." Advising and mentoring our children sends the message that we believe in them. Even a simple act such as helping them with their homework is a gesture of believing in them. When my kids brought home report cards, my wife and I never jumped all over them about a low grade. We discussed why a grade might have dropped and how it might be improved. We showed that we believed they could do better and encouraged them always to do their best. We offered constant reinforcement in our actions and words: "You can do it. We believe in you."

We also tried to attend all of our children's games, plays, and other performances when they were in school. We now do the same for our grandchildren's events. Everyone in the stands is cheering, but the cheers of parents and grandparents mean the most to children. Knowing we are cheering them on builds their confidence and tells them—simply by the fact we took the time and made the effort to be there—that we believe in them. "I believe in you"—whether conveyed by our actions, our attitudes, or our words—was ingrained in their upbringing.

I've carried over a similar philosophy with the members of the Orlando Magic. Despite their talents and great success as professional athletes, they are still young men who appreciate support and encouragement. As the owner of the Orlando Magic, I speak to the players often and attend all the games I can. My presence alone says, "I believe in you." I encourage them to be their best every day in every game. A point I emphasize to them is that "there is only one night for some." In each game they are playing for people who might be attending their first and maybe only NBA basketball game. These fans came to see a quality performance and watch elite basketball players.

So we want our players to perform to the best of their abilities in each game all season long—because they likely will not have a second chance to be their best for the person who may have come to watch their favorite player only one night. That thought applies to all of us each day. We may only have one chance to perform in ways that leave a positive impression. We may not get a second chance to tell people "I believe in you" or act in a way that lets them know they are important to us. If we miss that opportunity, it's gone.

I also want our players to know that I care for them and believe in them as individuals off the basketball court. My wife and I invite the Magic players, coaches, and staff to our home. Some of our children and grandchildren join us. Simply hosting them at our home with our family lets them know that we consider them family and that we believe in them and care for them like family. Fans see NBA players for their talents on the court, for their salaries in the millions of dollars, and as they're featured in national media. But these players also are young men—some barely beyond their teens.

Some of these players are suddenly millionaires at the age of twenty for whom the NBA may be their first job. So I counsel them about the importance of investing and saving their money, because an NBA career is relatively short. I speak to them about the importance of acceptable conduct. They've spent countless hours and days in the gym developing their talents and perfecting their skills. The last thing they should do is throw it away through thoughtless misconduct. I advise them to stay away from the wrong people and wrong places and to be home before midnight. That always gets a little laugh. But I point out that whenever the misconduct of a professional athlete is reported, the incident typically occurs after midnight and in a venue where the player should not have been.

We also show people we believe in them when we support their endeavors or causes. People who create and build are those who believe in themselves, but they need the support of other believers to fire their enthusiasm and passion, especially in the face of naysayers and doubters. Helen's and my philanthropy through our foundation is a gesture of "I believe in you." When we or any donor provide a lead gift to a project, that gift speaks louder than any publicity campaign. That donation sends a message to the community and other potential donors that a prominent person believes enough in the project to support it financially. Suddenly that project or organization has been backed by a big believer who adds validity to the cause. And in my experience, when Helen and I demonstrate our belief in a cause, other donors step up to help.

Our church denomination more than a century ago founded Rehoboth, a Christian school for mostly Native American students in New Mexico. A Rehoboth education helps students — many of whom come from low-income, poverty-level families — to develop confidence and grow not only intellectually but also emotionally and spiritually. These are students who need to believe in God, in themselves, and in the ability to achieve better lives for themselves. Helen and I have been privileged to be among the supporters of this cause for many years. We were honored to attend the dedication ceremony of Rehoboth's new sports and fitness center, a building that we and many other donors helped make happen. We were privileged to have the opportunity to show these students by our presence that we believe in them and demonstrate to the teachers and staff that we believe in their cause.

"I believe in you" also can help build a community and rally its members to greatness. I've tried whenever I could to inspire people in my community to achieve great things by assuring them "I believe in you." Downtown Grand Rapids has been reborn in the past forty years. Our nearly abandoned downtown of the past today is flourishing with a new skyline and the sight of buildings rising every day. I've worked to be a community leader in this effort and hope I've helped by telling these community builders "I believe in you" to get the job done. Whenever I'm asked to speak at a building dedication, to a business group, or at a fund-raising dinner, I try to incorporate this same message in my words to the community: "I believe in you." My hope is that they leave motivated to believe that they can be achievers, that they have a wonderful community and live in a great state and country. I want each one of them to believe that he or she can contribute to our greatness and that each plays an important role.

I've found that even a president of the United States can use a little encouragement at times to know people believe in him. Whenever I was in Washington, D.C., when Gerald Ford was president, I'd call the White House to see if he might have a little time to chat. His appointments secretary would often say encouragingly, "He'd love to see you. He needs to see someone from his hometown and someone who's not looking for a handout." As U.S. president, Gerald Ford had the responsibility of making huge decisions affecting millions of people. I did what I could just by dropping in for visits to reinforce that I was behind him and believed in him and to let him know when I thought people in the heartland of our nation agreed with him on major issues.

Even though we don't have the weight of the Free World

on our shoulders, we all need to be encouraged in our daily work by an employer or coworker who believes we can do the job well. My businesses have employed thousands of people. To succeed they need to work in an atmosphere of believing in people and their talents. We recently had a meeting for the staff in which one of the speakers was our new food and beverage manager. He shared with the staff some of his background and how he has succeeded in his career. He started out washing pots and pans and worked his way to one of the top positions in his profession. He had to know when he was washing pots and pans that someone believed in him, and he had to believe in himself.

Believing in the dishwashers and others in some of the lowest positions often pays the highest dividends. Believing in people who are at the top of their game is easy. We also need to believe in people who need a lift. Many years ago, Amway bought the Mutual Broadcasting System. We hired Larry King to do a late-night talk show. Larry had a regional show in Florida but had been away from radio for about three years. We were the first ones to bring him back to radio. The man who ran our network at that time had worked with Larry King in Florida and said he was really a great talk-show host.

He told us, "If you're willing to give him a chance, I have an idea for an all-night show on our radio network starting at midnight and running till 5:00 A.M." So we put Larry on and opened the telephone lines—one of the first shows ever to do so. People called in, and Larry started doing what became his signature talk-show and interview style.

I was honored whenever Larry invited me to be a guest on his show. He would say to me, "Come on down. We need a conservative on the show. I get a lot of liberals down here but can't get the conservatives. They don't want to stay up that late." He later went on to the big time, but he was with us for many years. Larry King is a great guy, and I feel good that we gave him his first opportunity for a major radio talk show and believed in him.

Believing in ourselves and others is a critical element in the amazing human achievements we see every day and may take for granted. Just consider, for example, the celebration in my home state of the fiftieth anniversary in 2007 of the Mackinac Bridge, which spans five miles of the straits of Lakes Michigan and Huron between Michigan's lower and upper peninsulas. The designers of the bridge had to believe in their design for this huge suspension bridge, the engineers had to believe the bridge would withstand gale-force winds and tons of vehicles, and the workers had to believe all the cement they were pouring and cable they were stringing would one day become the bridge they saw on the drawing board. Developing a positive attitude stems from this single-yet-powerful word "believe" and really feeling it in your whole being.

This is something I wrote in *Believe!* in 1975 and that I still embrace today: "I believe that one of the most powerful forces in the world is the will of people who believe in themselves, who dare to aim high, to go confidently after the things that they want from life." So I made it my mission to tell people in *Believe!* and in speech after speech that in essence, "I believe in you." I told them I believed in a God of unlimited potential who empowers people to reach their dreams. Jay and I had to overcome a number of challenges, none of which ever stopped us from believing. If we had listened to all the naysayers and weighed the logical reasons against us, we never would have attempted to start an air service or a drive-in restaurant or Amway. Imagine your impact on the lives of people to whom you say, "I believe in you." You're not simply complimenting them or thanking them for a job well done or past achievements. You're saying you have faith in their abilities to achieve something that is yet to be done—even if it's something they may never have done and even if they doubt themselves.

I've told our Amway distributors countless times that their mission is to lift up people and that the first fundamental of that mission is a belief in people. When Jay and I were asked how we came up with our business and its principles we answered that it started with the fundamental belief that people have value. When we started, the conventional wisdom seemed to be: "People don't want to work; they're lazy, indifferent; they want to live on Social Security or collect unemployment." We disagreed, saying we believe people are worthy and want to work and get ahead. Ever since, I've emphasized that it's nearly impossible to build a business if you think people are no good.

When Norman Vincent Peale was encouraged by his college professor to believe in himself, he said the professor also told him to believe that God would help him. Peale said he walked out of the college building and down a broad flight of stairs. On the fourth step from the bottom he stopped. After seventy years he still remembered distinctly which step he was on and his prayer. "Lord," he prayed, "you can take a drunk and make him sober; you can change a thief into an honest person. Can't you also take a poor mixed-up guy like me and make him normal?" He said that was the start of a series of miracles that turned him into a believer in himself and a positive thinker.

The ability to create an atmosphere of belief is a skill we need in our leaders today. As I've said, learning to be positive and learning to use positive phrases is especially important for leaders. We need more leaders who can express what they believe in and impart their beliefs to others who will join them. Some have said of me that I'm not selling products; I'm selling *you* on *you*. Maybe that's because I've seen so many people who have made a choice to be confident. They start with uncertainty and a lack of belief in themselves, but with each little success they begin to believe a little more. They eventually discover talents and abilities they never knew they possessed.

When we talk about believing, we also need to mention the need to try. We never know what we can accomplish until we test our beliefs by trying. Most of what I've tried in life worked because I believed in it and committed myself to try it. Back in 1987, a fellow yachtsman asked me to help the New York Yacht Club regain the America's Cup from Australia. I was cochairman of the *America II* syndicate. (The boat was named *America II* after the *America*, which first won the cup in England in 1851.) Amway also was one of three sponsors of the team, so I had a lot at stake. We didn't win, but in defeat I kept a positive message. As I told the news media that asked for my reaction, "If you don't enter the race, you'll never win. That's how life works. Even though we didn't win, we entered and competed."

I also gave success a chance to happen, not giving up because I wasn't an overnight success. Believing in yourself doesn't always mean you have a vision. We started Amway in a basement. We didn't know how our first products would sell. We didn't know how the sales plan would ultimately work. We didn't start with a big factory. But after a few people started selling a little and sharing the opportunity, we finally built a one-hundred-by-forty-three-foot building. Great vision we had! Did we think Amway was going to be a huge business someday? Who are you kidding? We bought two acres for that building and were able to get two more, which we thought we'd never need but could use for a parking lot.

The point is, you can try or cry. My father never let me say "can't." The opposite of "can't" is "try." When you believe in yourself, you can visualize the person you have the potential to be. You can devote yourself totally to achieving your goals when you break the crying habit and absolutely believe in what you can do. Then you'll also have the confidence to inspire others to believe in themselves. "I believe in you" is an inspirational phrase for leaders to use, for parents to tell their children or grandchildren, for a friend in need who is going through a tough time, for students to hear from teachers, and for employees to hear from employers.

We can start to set our communities and country on a positive course by making a conscious decision to believe in ourselves and each other. I believe that America is the greatest country in the world and that our future depends on all Americans' sharing that belief. We need to believe in the work we're doing or find a different job. We must believe that our nation affords unlimited potential to achieve our dreams and then we must pursue our goals.

Norman Vincent Peale had a conversion on that fourth step from the bottom that he remembered seventy years later. Because his new condition made him so happy, he became concerned with those who were not and decided to devote his life to writing and preaching. He had become a believer, and never doubted again. You don't have to be a Norman Vincent Peale. Just think of who you might set on a new course simply by showing someone you believe in him or her or learning to use the powerful phrase, "I believe in you."

5

"I'm proud of you"

Like all grandparents, I always loved to watch my grandchildren at play.

One day children are concentrating on trying to take their first step, and, before we know it, they have the command of their growing bodies to run and jump, ride a bicycle, hit a baseball, dive into a pool, and perform on stage.

As I've watched my grandchildren play, it's been natural for them to try to get my attention and acknowledgment. Years ago at the pool, it struck me that as each of them dove or went down the slide, they would call out, "Watch me, Grandpa!" As each tried to outdo the other, they looked my way to be sure I was watching.

"Watch me!" Children long for someone they love to watch them and offer an approving smile or affirming words. And as they grow up, they long for their parents and grandparents to watch them get good grades, play sports, play in bands, act in plays, and go off to college. You've surely noticed this in your own children and grandchildren. Probably the most powerful thing we can say to our kids, next to "I love you," is "I'm proud of you."

But "Watch me" is not just kid's stuff. Our desire as children expressed in "Watch me" remains with us for a lifetime — a human need to be recognized and acknowledged by those who mean the most to us. Simply put, we want to feel that they are proud of us. We long for recognition all our lives. We work hard to earn the right to be proud of ourselves. As wonderful as it is to take pride in our accomplishments, the power of that feeling is multiplied manyfold when others go out of their way to announce to us, "I'm proud of you."

I'm fortunate to know Bill Hybels, the founding and senior pastor of Willow Creek Community Church near Chicago and author of several Christian books. An enjoyable afternoon on a sailboat was an opportunity for him to catch me up on all the positive energy and activity at his church. At home after our sail, I took a moment to jot him a note letting him know how proud I was of him. He later told me he kept that note for weeks. Imagine that! Bill is recognized nationally by millions yet he was touched by a simple line of encouragement from me.

My wife, Helen, received the 2007 Lifetime Achievement

Award from the Grand Rapids Symphony for her many years of volunteering to help develop a first-class orchestra and give the gift of music to our community. My children and I bought ads in the program that included the simple words "We're proud of you." Helen needed no compensation for her work with the symphony. She volunteered because of her love of music and her community. But I know a few loving words of recognition from her family were priceless.

Behind a lot of hard work is a simple desire to be recognized as the best in our profession, to be given a more impressive job title, to win an award or see our name in the paper. Everyone appreciates a pat on the back, an "Attaboy!" or a "You go girl!" I learned quickly in business to appreciate the power of recognizing achievement and how quickly unrecognized achievement can kill incentive. Only saints toil for long in anonymity. When you learn to look for positive things in the lives of others you'll find it's easy to tell them you're proud of them. God created each one of us as a unique individual with our own talents and dreams. He's instilled in each of us an awareness that we're special and are here for a purpose. Recognition encourages our God-given desire to do our best. That's not to say we should be arrogant or should not heed the proverb that pride comes before a fall. But let's rejoice with pride that, as the Bible tells us, we are "wonderfully made" and capable of achieving wonderful things.

The business I started in 1959 with Jay Van Andel was very simple. People could start their own Amway business and earn income simply by selling products to people they knew and met, plus income from the sales of people they sponsored into the business. People who signed up received a kit with the products and instructions needed to get started. Amway is a business of people, and people need recognition to succeed. So we built into our business various levels of achievement and opportunities for achievers to be recognized onstage at sales meetings in front of their peers. Built right into our business was a way for people to say to others in their organization, "Watch me." And people whom they looked up to and admired in the business had a built-in way to say, "I'm proud of you."

Is it powerful? Judging from the thousands of people I've seen achieve beyond their dreams, I'd say it's life-changing. "I'm proud of you" doesn't only have the power to recognize achievement. That little phrase is concentrated power—an energy boost to encourage people to do more than they thought possible. That's another reason Jay and I built recognition into our business. We actually laid both recognition and rewards into the foundation, because we had learned that reward alone does not have the strength to motivate people to achieve their full potential and dreams. We had two solid footings: levels for financial rewards and levels of recognition designated by precious jewels, such as Pearl, Emerald, and Diamond. Now, a lot of people might think a jewel designation is insignificant and that the big motivator is financial rewards—going after the money, buying the house and car. Who wants to work hard to earn a Pearl or Diamond pin?

But we found that the status of achieving the level of Diamond was as important—if not more important—in motivating people to achieve. Diamond achievers in our business had their photo in the company magazine and were recognized onstage in front of thousands of their fellow businesspeople. That recognition, the cheers from their peers, and the congratulations from their leaders conveyed in a very big way the very powerful message "I'm proud of you."

After writing my third book, *Hope From My Heart: Ten Lessons for Life*, I came up with an idea for using the book to recognize people whose actions give hope to others. Whenever our local newspaper ran a story about an inspiring achievement or a volunteer making a difference in our community, I'd send that person a copy of the book along with a note. My note congratulated them and said that we had something in common as people who try to give others hope. I get lots of notes back from these people thanking me for the book and saying they plan to keep the letter in an honored place

For all the phrases in this book, I'd like to emphasize that beyond just saying them you must consider putting them in writing. It only takes a minute to write a note. But it's a powerful act of inspiration and encouragement. I've seen notes from me posted on people's refrigerators and even framed. That's an example of the power in saying in so many words, "I'm proud of you." Putting the phrase in writing just adds more power. I said years ago, when people were embracing the rush of digital conveniences from compact discs to email, that I was still much more an analog than a digital person. I grew up with rotary phones, radios filled with tubes instead of chips, and "snail" mail. I appreciate the speed and convenience of email. But nothing conveys a word of thanks or an expression of concern like a note written on paper, tucked into a hand-addressed envelope, and dropped into the mail. Remember how you felt the last time you received a small, hand-addressed envelope and opened it to find inside a card of thanks or congratulations? I believe even the most important, busiest executive who is flooded daily with emails and other business mail will stop to open such a card.

Because I travel extensively, I've found it much more practical to fly private planes. I've had occasion to provide rides to friends. Barbara Bush has never traveled on a plane of mine without sending a handwritten note of thanks. Barbara is a note-writer. And I treasure her for that and for the notes she writes. Her son, George W., does it, too. Many years ago, when the Amway method of business was still widely misunderstood, I was a guest on the *Phil Donahue Show.* Mr. Donahue and some members of his audience were critical of me and the business. I did the best I could to defend myself against a well-prepared professional interviewer and an antagonistic group throwing questions at me on national television. After the show, when we were trying to sort out what kind of impression I made and what kind of job I had done on behalf of Amway and our distributors, I received a note from Barbara Bush with this simple message: "DeVos 10, Donahue 0." You can imagine how that lifted my spirits! Now that truly conveys "I'm proud of you" with impact!

Because the power of these simple phrases is magnified when sent in writing, sending them in a letter or note is well worth the extra effort. And a simple note need not take a lot of time. I'd recommend keeping a supply of blank note cards or thank-you cards with stamps at the ready. You don't have to be a poet or compose lengthy letters. All that's required is a simple sentiment from the heart that will fit on a small card. The next time you think of thanking that special someone, you can quickly and easily put your thoughts into action. That way, you'll make sure you recognize the people who did a great job, or who may need a word of encouragement, or who just need to know someone is thinking of them. I'm convinced that this, one of the smallest investments we can make, can generate some of the most powerful results.

We all need encouraging gestures of "I'm proud of you"—whether in words, notes, or actions—and no matter if we're just starting out in life or business and trying to build our confidence or if we've risen to the top. We needed it as kids from our parents, as students from our teachers and coaches, and still need affirmation as adults from our coworkers and supervisors.

I've given hundreds of speeches. I'm asked to speak to motivate and encourage the audience, and I'm proud and honored by the privilege. Early in my speaking days I would ask Helen after a speech to tell me how she thought I did. I was looking for approval from the person who means the most in my life. Helen would give me the affirmation I needed. But I remember at times in those early days asking her more than once about my performance—always fishing for a few more compliments; for Helen to be proud of me meant more than a standing ovation.

I find that "I'm proud of you" is especially uplifting for people who typically don't win the awards and rewards of life, who may doubt their abilities and have a tough time finding something to be proud about. That's why it's doubly important for parents and teachers and employers to find ways to say, "I'm proud of you." I can speak from experience. I was not an honor student in school. In fact, my father refused to continue paying my tuition at my Christian high school because I was goofing off and not focusing on my schoolwork. My Latin teacher gave me a D on the condition I'd never take her class again. I eventually decided to work toward better grades, but I never got all As. I once admitted this in a commencement speech to a class of high school students. Many of them were on the honor roll or had received national awards. More than half the class was recognized at these graduation ceremonies with colored tassels that were hung around their necks as academic awards. They likely heard "I'm proud of you" several times that day from parents and teachers.

So I felt it important in my remarks to focus on the students without honors. Odds were that few of these students heard the powerful words "I'm proud of you" on their graduation day. They probably felt like they were just another number as they watched the honor students receive their awards. I encouraged them by telling them that every member of the graduating class could accomplish great things for the Kingdom of God. I hope my words helped send them off from high school with the thought that the world also held promise for them and that they, too, had talents that could help them achieve their dreams.

That's the kind of encouragement that young people remember for a lifetime. My son Doug can still recall some simple words of encouragement from me that he says helped him in elementary school. I was driving him to school one day when he admitted to me that he was having trouble making friends. I encouraged him to be happy. "People like being around happy people," I told him. Doug remembers getting out of the car at school and hearing me call after him, "Go get 'em, Mr. Happy!"

Doug is now grown, a husband, and the father of four, but to this day he remembers that ride to school and my words of encouragement. In fact, the tradition continues. One of Doug's daughters made her high school freshman football team as a placekicker—one of few girls to ever play on a boy's high school team. I enjoy going to her games and cheering her on. For a girl to try out for a boy's football team surely took a lot of courage and confidence—likely instilled by her parents' encouraging words as she was growing up.

Helen had an opposite experience growing up. Her mother,

fearing the worst, did not let her ride a bike or swim. Her family had spent several summers near the Atlantic Ocean, and they lived close to Lake Michigan, giving Helen plenty of opportunities to swim, but her mother kept her close to the shore. With my encouragement, although still not a swimmer, Helen has learned to snorkel (with a life vest), and, knowing her childhood experience, it's been wonderful to see her enjoy snorkeling in waters around the world. Encouraging our loved ones by expressing our pride in them gets them off the beach and exploring the depths.

Can a few simple words have the power to make a positive impact? Find a reason to tell your children you're proud of them, and see for yourself. "I'm proud of you" is most powerful when said to someone in public, in front of people they respect and admire—their parents, friends, teachers, supervisors, or esteemed colleagues. I once was privileged to chat over dinner with a world-renowned brain surgeon from New York City who came to lecture at the Helen DeVos Children's Hospital in Grand Rapids. He complimented me on the hospital. "In a few years," he said, "you'll be able to attract the best and brightest physicians from around the country." I told him, "Look around. A lot of the best and brightest are already here."

Years later, our chief of pediatric hematology and oncology

told me he'd heard our conversation from the next table. He said my words of pride were like a huge pat on the back for him. He is proud to be a member of a talented team of physicians. And he said that just hearing me express my pride in his team to an esteemed member of his profession made him thankful from the bottom of his heart.

That warms my heart. I want to be a cheerleader in life, because we unfortunately already have our fair share of people who go the opposite direction: tearing down instead of building up. That's why we have to believe in unlimited potential and encourage others to do likewise. How will they ever know if they can paint that picture, run that business, sell that product, write that book, earn that degree, hold that office, make a speech, win that game—unless they try it? Feeling comfortable saying "I'm proud of you" to anyone who excels in any endeavor is simply a matter of having respect for the dignity of all people. I've been told I can relate to everyone from presidents to parking lot attendants. I'm proud of that. My father was an electrician and was out of work during the Great Depression. But that doesn't mean I wasn't proud of him. He worked hard to raise my sisters and me and encouraged me to be a business owner.

Many years ago I attended a symposium on vocational education with men who had doctorate degrees and years of experience in learning. I sat through their comments about out-of-work laborers, such as, "Maybe we can at least make a good carpenter out of him," or, "Well, he'll still be just a plumber, but . . ." I also was the speaker that evening. So I had the opportunity to remind these men that they were looking down from their Ph.D. towers and trying to find a niche in society for the poor fellows who in their opinions were not bright enough to go to college.

I don't believe anyone is *just* a mechanic or *just* a salesman, *just* a trash hauler, or just anything. We're all human beings with dignity, made in the image of God Himself and using the talents He has given us to contribute to society in our own special way. Respect is the key. And with respect, we can say "I'm proud of you" to anyone for a job well done.

If you're a parent, you have the greatest opportunity to say "I'm proud of you" to your children and an opportunity to have the greatest impact on a person's future success. If you're an employer, teacher, or coach, I encourage you to make "I'm proud of you" part of your daily vocabulary. I believe each of us was created to achieve a potential. You can help people you know or love reach their full potential by looking for ways you can express your pride in them.

Within each person you meet is a bit of that child or grandchild looking for approval and saying, "Watch me." Are you watching? Do you notice the achievements — small or large — of your family members, friends, neighbors, and coworkers or employees? You can help them grow by telling them, "I'm proud of you!"

6

"Thank you"

Remember when you were little

and an adult gave you a piece of candy or small gift? One of your parents likely prompted you with, "What do you say?" They were, of course, trying to get you to say "Thank you." If you're a parent, you hope that your child will remember his manners by saying "Thank you" when someone gives him a present and not embarrass you by simply grabbing it without a word and running away.

Responsible parents are adamant about teaching their children to say "Thank you." Having "Thank you" in our vocabulary and top of mind is simply an expectation for all of us who function successfully in our civilized society. Store clerks are expected to thank us for our business. When a server brings our meal, we typically say "Thank you." "Thank you" is the appropriate and expected response when someone pays us a compliment about our new suit or doing a great job. We automatically should say thanks when someone makes us dinner, gives us a ride, or presents us with a gift.

"Thank you" is an acknowledgment of the other person's generosity. It recognizes the other person's kindness and the effort that person made to think of us. "Thank you" says we appreciate a job well done and the time someone devoted to develop his or her talents to perform for us or provide a skilled service.

When we completed our world headquarters building at Amway Corp., we held a dedication with then–U.S. Representative Gerald Ford, the township supervisor, local business leaders, and other dignitaries. Even before this high-level dedication, however, we held another special event.

We hosted an open house for all the skilled laborers who built it. All these dedicated and talented workers—the men and women who drew the blueprints, erected the steel girders, placed the brick, installed the windows, built the roof, laid the carpet, and hung the drapes—enjoyed the party we provided and a chance to see the results of their hard work. Rarely at that time did construction workers get the opportunity to see their completed product. So we invited them to see the finished building and took the opportunity to shake their hands, have a little conversation and, most important, say "Thank you." And they appreciated it. They were a bit surprised at the invitation to such an event, which we hosted simply to say "Thank you."

The rarity of this type of event speaks volumes about our tendency sometimes to overlook thanking people. Why is it that thanking certain people never crosses our minds? When problems arise in a construction project, we're quick to complain. But when a project goes smoothly and without a hitch, we tend to take the workers and their expertise for granted. In 2007 we built the JW Marriott Hotel in downtown Grand Rapids on time, without injury, without lost production time, and without a major hitch. All levels of skilled labor and contractors did their jobs well and fulfilled their obligations. Workers arrived on time each day, worked till the end of the day, and went home to their families likely feeling a great sense of pride in contributing their special talents to such a significant project. These are the people we make sure we acknowledge when we have a dedication ceremony. As I've mentioned before, I also make sure I acknowledge the work of the various staff members in our hotels and convention center who easily could be overlooked but who are there to deliver a meal on time or provide service with a smile after a long day.

In my business, employees received a Christmas gift each year. The employees could choose a gift from a catalog, simply because they were employees of the company and for no other reason than that it was Christmas and we wanted to let them know they were appreciated. It's amazing how even the smallest gesture of thanks has incredible power to make people feel needed and valued. Even within families, when we become familiar with one another and may tend to get casual about manners, we still should remember to say "Thank you." It's a habit we ingrained in our children that continues around our family dinner table and one we insist on from our grand-children.

Saying thanks and gestures of thanks are expressions of our love or kind thoughts about an individual. Whenever we give even a small gift, the saying really is true that "it's the thought that counts." But what's most important is that we put our thoughts into action with a gesture: a card, a gift, or any expression of "Thank you. I appreciate you. You do good work and that work helped me."

Just feeling thankful does nothing to demonstrate our gratitude. Too often, we think about saying thanks but somehow don't get around to taking the time. Unfortunately, that school-teacher whom we liked and appreciated may get through the entire school year without a thank-you—never knowing that someone appreciated her talents and efforts. We might have thought about it but never gotten around to visiting the classroom or picking up the phone or sending a card or small gift.

A demonstration of our gratitude can be as simple as saying "Thank you" or can be more elaborate. When made for the right reason, more elaborate gestures of thanks can do wonders. Many years ago, when I was on the board of Grand Valley State University in our community, there was a discussion about how to raise more money for the university's foundation. I offered the idea that the best way was to honor people. So we started honoring people for their contributions both to the university and to the community. We made them guests of honor at banquets and presented them with an award and hung an artist's portrait of them in university buildings. That became our tradition of saying "Thank you" to various people. They might be prominent professors or community members who were significant to the university. We said "Thank you" by honoring them publicly. Today social calendars in Grand Rapids are filled with such events that honor people for their contributions. We have black-tie gala dinners with prominent guest speakers that fill banquet halls. These are fund-raisers that make money for their organizations and encourage more donors to support the cause, but they also honor people who deserve a significant gesture of gratitude.

Jay and I were honored in 1999 in celebration of our thirty years of economic contributions to revitalizing downtown Grand Rapids. The fund-raising event was titled "Thanks for the Renaissance, Jay and Rich," and our hometown paid tribute to us for "the tireless efforts and extraordinary generosity of two men who have played major roles in the renaissance of Grand Rapids' downtown district and the small businesses that have flourished as a result." During those thirty years we were happy to help the city in which we grew up, and the time flew by without our worrying about being thanked. But being on the receiving end of such an elaborate demonstration of gratitude helped crystallize for me the power of being thanked and thanking others. I admit that I enjoyed being thanked.

People like to be thanked and they *need* to be thanked! The well of kindness can dry up when we fail to acknowledge the givers of gifts. Some people contribute significantly because they believe in a cause or from the goodness of their hearts. It takes relatively little in return to thank them. I later was raising funds for what now is the Cook DeVos Health Sciences Building of Grand Valley State University. I struck up a conversation with an elderly gentleman whom I met in the parking lot of the health building. He was in his nineties but looked much younger in his beautiful shirt and tie and bright blue sport coat. I said to him, "You look like a million dollars!"

I ran into him again inside the building and realized he was one of the potential donors for our fund-raising efforts. So I said to him, "You look like a million dollars, but I'm really here to ask you for a million dollars. We're naming each floor of this building for donors who give a million dollars, and I'd appreciate your support." He said he would contribute. I told him I also had another amount in mind for the contribution required to have the entire building named for him. His grandson, who was with him, overheard the conversation and said, "Grandpa, don't forget your grandchildren." As I spoke with him further and listened to his story of how he had made his money, I realized that hardly anybody in town knew about him. They didn't know how he started or how he built a huge business. I decided we needed to do more than simply name each floor. We needed to do something to inspire students by the stories of the donors so they would know the person behind the names. Often buildings on campuses are named for donors, but the students know nothing about the individual beyond a name. The university came up with the idea of having a glass showcase on each floor with exhibits and mementos inside that illustrate each donor's story.

Students now can stop to look and say, "So that's what that man did, and that's why he's here and why this floor is named for him." It was a wonderful way to say "Thank you."

There are all sorts of creative ways that need not be that elaborate when you begin to think about how you can honor someone and say "Thank you" for his or her impact on your life. The personal thank-you letters and notes are never to be disregarded, but there are other ways to say "Thank you," whether you are a businessperson, a religious leader, a parent, or someone in another leadership role.

You might thank your children for working hard in school and give them something special for a good report card or celebrate when they graduate from high school or college. A thank-you might be treating them to a special day or weekend. Time is the most valuable gift a parent can give. I remember being busy building the business and Doug, who was maybe twelve years old at the time, telling me, "You're never home." I said, "I am, too. I'm home a lot." He said, "Just a minute, I'll go get a calendar." He had a calendar on the back of a cupboard door in the kitchen with an X on all the days I'd been gone. Talk about an eye-opener! So, yes, the gift of time is a most valuable gift. Doug's calendar opened my eyes to the importance of simply being home and involved in his life. One way I tried to make time for my children while busy traveling on business was to take them with me. I would take one child along on most overseas trips. My oldest son, Dick, took the first trip to Australia, and then each child in turn went with us for a two- or three-week trip. Their teachers didn't always appreciate it, but my wife and I felt these trips were wonderful educational opportunities as well as great one-on-one time with our children.

In addition to thanking the people we appreciate or who have done us a service or kindness, we also need to adjust our attitude to one of being thankful. We have been greatly blessed in this country, and too often we tend to take our blessings for granted. "I thank you." We can never wear out that phrase. It should always be on the tip of our tongue if we are truly grateful to others who help us each day and to God who has richly blessed us with more abundance and freedom than any country in history. When thinking about whom to add to our thank-you list, we need to remember each day to thank God in prayer for the abundance of His blessings.

We're often too slow to give thanks and too quick to complain. Maybe we're so focused on ourselves and busy with our lives that we forget to give thanks. Or maybe it's because we in America have become complacent with a level of luxury and leisure beyond the imagination of much of the world's population.

We tend to take our blessings for granted, like the story about a homeowner who hired a real estate agent to prepare an ad to sell his home. The homeowner was reading the ad in the paper about his home's many attractive features. He called the real estate agent to say he no longer wished to sell. When asked what changed his mind, the homeowner said, "After reading your ad, I realized I already live in the house I always wanted to live in."

As Norman Vincent Peale preached for many years, if you're worried about your problems and finding difficulty focusing on the positive, "Get Out of Yourself." Start thinking of others. Despite a list of blessings to count each day, we unfortunately can always find something to complain about. If we thought of someone much less fortunate and even helped that person, we would feel much more grateful for our own condition. Peale believed that truly great people live extraordinary lives because they have a habit of thinking about other people and showing them kindness. When we do a kindness for another person we can much better appreciate and be thankful to those who do us a kindness. We can sit down to a meal, for example, thinking only of how the food will satisfy our appetite, or we can stop to appreciate the thought, skill, and effort involved in preparing the meal and be thankful.

There's the old story about a group of farmers sitting around a potbelly stove in the general store during a winter storm and one says, "Well, you remember in 1970 we had that terrible drought and we lost all of our crops and everything burned up in the fields?" The other farmers nodded that they remembered. Another farmer said, "Remember in '84 all the crops were coming up good and then we didn't get any rain and everything burned up in the field?" And they all said they remembered that year, too. They all had their memories of years when things had gone wrong. Finally, one old farmer said, "Yeah, but don't forget '87. That was a terrific year. We had a great crop and everything went well. But it took a lot out of the soil."

Like that story, we at times find it difficult to be truly thankful. So, if you have children in school who are learning something new each day, thank their teachers. If you have fond memories of childhood and have grown into a productive adult, thank your parents. Thank your grandparents for their wisdom. Thank your employer for your job. The list goes on.

If you feel safe and secure in your home, community, and country, thank your neighbors, a police officer, or a member of the military. If you are uplifted by a Sunday sermon, thank your pastor. If your load at work was lightened a bit by a helping hand, thank that coworker.

Beyond saying "Thank you," adjust your attitude each day

to being thankful for the abundance of God's blessings. If you and your family are healthy, have a roof over your head, food on the table, clothes on your back, and the gifts of love, laughter, and leisure, give thanks to God for His many blessings. And don't forget to share a portion of His blessings with those who have far fewer blessings to count.

I believe in a daily attitude of thankfulness, of expressing thanks for even the smallest favor or consideration, of thanking God in prayer, and of showing my gratitude by sharing His abundance. I believe thankfulness is powerful and one of the keys to a more positive society.

7

"I need you"

My very life once depended on needing someone. At the age of seventy-one

I needed a heart transplant to stay alive. We called every heart center in the country, but because of my age no one would take me. So I not only desperately needed someone, I also needed an "it"—a new heart. My need finally was met by one person who agreed to take my case, Professor Sir Magdi Yacoub, a thoracic and cardiovascular surgeon at Harefield Hospital in London. I met with him in London because he first wanted to determine if I would be able to survive transplant surgery. He told me, "Before I'd go through this operation, knowing how much you'd have to endure and suffer, I need to know if you have the mental attitude and spirit to go through this."

What he was essentially asking was, "Do you have a reason to live?" Helen and two of our sons were with me—he could see three reasons right there! After further dialogue and assessment, he agreed to take me as a patient. Thank God he said yes, because I really needed him — the one person in the world who could possibly save my life. Fortunately, after five months of waiting I received my new heart. The transplant operation was another lesson in trusting the hand of God upon my life. For one to receive a heart at the age of seventy-one was impossible in the United States and rare in England. Just finding a surgeon willing to consider my case was incredible.

Another challenge could have been my rare blood type, which limited the odds of finding a donor with the same type. But my doctor said I was actually fortunate to have a rare AB blood type, because the hospital occasionally had hearts with my blood type that went unused. Without my rare blood type, I would not have had a chance of being a transplant candidate. Still, because I was a U.S. citizen, the donor heart would have to be one no United Kingdom transplant candidate could use. As a further complication, tests revealed that a donor heart would need an enlarged right ventricle to be suitable for my needs.

As I waited — growing weaker by the day — my cardiologist at the time, Emma Birk, found a donor. A woman in the same hospital needed a lung transplant, and surgeons typically prefer to transplant the lungs and heart as a unit. The hospital had located a heart and lungs for the woman from a victim of an auto accident. Her healthy heart would be surplus. *Precious* surplus. Even more miraculous, her lung problem had contributed to the development of a larger-than-normal right ventricle. God certainly is in the details.

Only the spiritually blind could fail to see the hand of God in my circumstances. Ultimately, there is only one explanation for this miracle. The grace of God. Just as I needed Dr. Yacoub, someone is counting on you. Someone *needs you*. Each of us is needed. Believe it. And tell others—your spouse, your children, your employees or coworkers, your garbage man or pastor—"I need you."

"There's no I in TEAM." I hear that a lot among people in the Amway business. Amway is a "we" business. The business is built on the principle of the success of each individual contributing to the success of the whole. Each person's success is to varying degrees dependent on the success of every other person. Those who have achieved the most are those who sponsor the greatest achievers. So the phrase "I need you" is one I've used often and one I've found to be powerful in motivating positive people. We all need to know we are needed. And it's the rare person who can make it through life without needing someone else.

Think of all the people you need or have needed in your

life: your parents, your spouse, your teammates and coworkers who made it possible for you to win or to finish a job, that true friend who may have been the only person around during a time of great need, that special teacher or coach who showed you the way, a police officer or firefighter in time of danger, the plumber when the pipe broke, your pastor when your spirits were low, your neighbor when you ran out of a key ingredient in the middle of fixing dinner, your insurance agent after your car accident, or your doctor who provided care. Most of us give little or no thought to farmers or even to where food comes from or to utility employees until we flip a switch and get no light or don't receive the stream of clean water that routinely comes from turning a faucet.

When I used to awake on winter mornings and discover all the streets had been plowed, I knew workers had been up all night to make the roads passable. When I flew into our airport in Grand Rapids on wintry nights and heard the reassuring voice saying to our pilots, "You're cleared for your approach," I knew that the airport crew was doing its job. The 9/11 terrorist attacks reminded all of us that our firefighters and police officers risk their lives to protect us, and yet they had been routinely doing this job without our giving them much thought.

Our current world situation also has been a reminder of the dedicated men and women who serve in our military. They do a remarkable job. Many years ago I was privileged to be aboard the aircraft carrier USS *Constellation* on maneuvers near San Diego. I watched as the crew conducted night flight operations on that huge ship, and I could not believe what I was seeing. Highly skilled and trained naval officers were performing precision takeoffs and landings in jet fighters costing tens of millions of dollars. They were preparing for the possibility that one day they and their sophisticated aircraft would need to defend the sea lanes essential to the flow of vital foreign materials on which our nation depends.

I think of "I need you" whenever I fly. As a licensed pilot and someone who travels frequently on private planes, I'm familiar with the traffic-control system that keeps aircraft from colliding—especially when crossing the Atlantic. Radar is not available on ocean crossings, so even the most competent pilots are totally dependent on air traffic controllers. Pilots must routinely report to air traffic controllers their positions at established checkpoints over the Atlantic. Their planes are surrounded by other aircraft ahead, behind, and below them. The pilots cannot see the other planes, but because all the pilots are reporting their positions and the time they reach each checkpoint, the air traffic controllers know each plane's position.

Planes flying over the Atlantic fly on different tracks—rather like invisible highways in the sky. When you're on a flight from New York to Paris, for example, there is likely—unbeknownst to you and unseen—a plane a thousand feet directly overhead, another below you, and others ahead and behind you. When I fly, often an air traffic controller will direct me to ascend to a higher or lower track so a plane behind me can pass. Without air traffic control, there would be nothing to prevent the plane above from descending into you or the plane behind from coming up too fast from the rear. All this maneuvering is achieved by air traffic controllers who guide hundreds of planes that leave the United States each afternoon and land at European airports in the morning and then guide them all back again.

The lives of millions of people can depend on the skills of a few people who are greatly needed. You also may know of individuals in your community who are needed. The activities in my community are great reminders of individuals we need. In 2000, for example, a committee was charged to come up with a project to commemorate the millennium. The decision was to transform a tract of land in an industrial district into a park that when completed will be larger in size than New York City's Central

Park. The park that we started, Millennium Park, today features a beach with a beach house, nature trails, picnic pavilions, children's play areas, and ponds for canoeing and fishing. Many ambitious plans remain on the drawing board to complete it. All this would not be possible without the diligence of a special volunteer. Peter Secchia, former U.S. ambassador to Italy and a well-known business owner and entrepreneur in our community, took on this project in his retirement—promoting the vision, raising funds, and working with government and businesses to help make the dream a reality. Two other prominent members of our community, David Frey and John Canepa, also have devoted their time and talents as volunteers.

These are examples of the kind of people we need. But consider: Without volunteers we'd have no one to make the fundraising calls or get out the vote for political campaigns; we'd have no volunteer fire departments, scout troops, or Little League teams. Look around your community and consider what would not exist without volunteers.

We need so many people that we tend to take them for granted. Think about the garbage man. Think of a world without people to haul away our trash. I've told this story before, but it bears repeating because it's the perfect example of "I need you." My family was staying at a cottage one summer where we had a wonderful garbage man. He was always prompt. You could set your watch by him. He didn't throw the trash cans or bang the lids. He made his rounds early in the morning and was respectful of people who were sleeping. One morning I was up at five-thirty when he arrived. I said to him, "I just wanted to tell you what a nice job you're doing and how much we need you around here." He just gave me a strange look and went on his way.

The next week I made a point of getting up early again and waiting for him. I watched him load my trash into his truck. I said, "You do a wonderful job. I just wanted you to know how much we need your valued service and appreciate what you do." He looked at me and asked, "Are you just getting in from a long night or getting a very early start to your day?" I explained that I'd gotten up just so I could let him know how much we valued the great job he was doing.

I saw him once again that summer and had a final chance to talk to him. He said, "I've been doing this job for twelve years and until now no one has ever recognized the value of what I was doing." How long could that community of cottages have survived if all the garbage was left to pile up all summer? We may not tell the people who collect our garbage, but we need them—just as we need so many other people whom we too often take for granted. It's important that we say, "I need you." I need you to solve this problem. I need you to work with us. We need you in this business. We really need you around here because you are an important part of our community. There is nothing wrong with learning to tell people that you are dependent upon them. Jay and I needed customers in our business. So we flat-out told them that we needed their business, that they were important to us.

When you look around there is no limit to all the people you need, but few of those people ever actually hear from you that you need them. We take them for granted and really don't think about them a lot. No one in a lofty position can say to someone in a lower position, "I don't need you." How successful would a company be that consisted of just presidents? The president of the company can't get to work in the winter if the person who drives the snowplow doesn't do his job. The executive washroom would be of little use without the contributions of the custodian. The enterprise would go broke quickly without people to make the products and maintain the machinery. Our families, schools, businesses, churches, communities—our whole society—are based on the fact that we need each other to survive. How many hermits do you know? Loners are rare and considered odd because so few of us can go without needing others in our lives. As Barbra Streisand sang in "People," "People who need people are the luckiest people in the world."

"I need you" is ingrained in our free society. I believe one reason our economy works is that people love being needed. We get a sense of purpose when we know we are needed each morning to open the store, deliver a product on time, or supervise employees. Think of all the professions that are filled by people who as part of their motivation want to be needed: teachers, police officers, firefighters, nurses, and doctors.

So I believe we all share a responsibility for encouraging people by acknowledging their contributions at every opportunity. People have asked me, "What is your job?" And I answer, "I'm a cheerleader." I just go around cheering people up. I encourage people. I run around and pat them on the back and tell them they're great. Amway was built on building people up. We were on a crusade of reminding people how great they are and that they can do far more than they ever thought they might do.

"I need you." That's such a powerful phrase for positive people because it acknowledges that each person is created by God, and God created each of us for a purpose and to fulfill a need. In America, each of us is free to use our God-given talents to fulfill those needs and to be needed. We are not surplus.

We're like the jet engine part that works with the others to keep the plane in the air; the musical instrument required to complete an orchestra; the eleventh player needed to field a winning football team.

When we know we are needed, we feel better about ourselves, perform better, and even want to do more to show how much we truly are needed. I have always enjoyed walking through our manufacturing plants at Amway. I'm amazed and fascinated by machinery and assembly lines designed to mix ingredients into household products, efficiently make boxes and bottles, fill those containers with powders or liquids, and seal and label the containers so they're ready for shipping to customers. But I'm more fascinated by the human mind that conceived this machinery and the people who constructed the parts and assembled the machines. And I'm most interested in our employees who work on the lines and in the plants and who show up for work on time each day and do their jobs well. A mile-long complex of manufacturing plants and offices hums along every working day because thousands of people get up and go to work. That goes on at thousands of businesses in America and around the world.

People who walk with me through our plants comment on the relationship I have with our employees. They remark on how I show an interest in them, am able to engage them in small talk, and how they step off the assembly line to shake my hand or look up from their work and with a wide grin call out, "Hi, Rich." I believe this relationship is built in large part on mutual need—we need them to do jobs vital to our business and they need us for their livelihoods. I let them know that without them not a single product could be manufactured or shipped that day. Our distributors need each one of them to build their businesses. I've demonstrated that I'm aware of the worth and value of each one of them, regardless of their job. I believe that each one of us on earth is a creature of God, that we are here for a purpose and worthy of respect as a human being.

Years ago I enjoyed being a guest on Larry King's late-night radio talk show based in Florida because I was interested in the varying opinions of people across the country who called in to express their views. While this was fascinating, I also unfortunately was exposed to a world of the disillusioned, discouraged, and disheartened. One caller said to me, "I don't know the difference between capitalism and communism. In one you're a slave to the state, and in the other you're a slave to the capitalist pigs. We're all slaves to somebody." I bled for him. His vision of history was distorted. He'd lost sight of the accomplishments of generations of free Americans. I thought at the time that his attitude reflected a fear of success and distrust of leadership. I also now believe that he never felt needed or had anyone to tell him he was appreciated. He felt like a slave instead of a human being with dignity whose contributions were acknowledged. I believe there still are many people out there who have the mistaken impression that they need to be slaves rather than free contributors to a better society and future. They desperately need to hear, "I need you."

As I reflect on my years of leadership, I know how important it is for leaders to be able to say or convey the message, "I need you." Anyone who becomes an effective leader and wins the respect and admiration of many followers knows that he or she needs them. The higher some leaders climb, the more they lose sight of the people they think they left behind and no longer need. That's a fatal mistake. Organizations in which people feel they are not needed are doomed to failure or at least a bumpy ride of uncertainty and dissatisfaction. None of us is too important or self-sufficient not to need other people. Why not create a more positive atmosphere in our homes, workplaces, and communities by telling people, "I need you"?

8

"I trust you"

A friend of mine once told me about his family's "Trust Medal." When children in his family reach the age of twenty-one, they are eligible for this trust medal. Earning it requires that they have had a good trustworthy relationship in the family and in the community. They have to earn the trust of their parents by living by rules and values and staying out of trouble. They earn the trust of their parents, who in turn endow the children with their trust. When family members gather for each child's twenty-first birthday, they present the trust medal and celebrate the achievement. That's a rather good idea, I thought, to demonstrate how family members can support each other in being trustworthy and to show how much they value trust in all their relationships.

"I trust you" is another very important powerful phrase for positive people. The success of our society depends on trusting that someone will do a good job, trusting each other to be honest, trusting that people will keep their promises. We need trust among coworkers and within our families. We trust our children, and they trust us. Many of us are given great responsibilities that are all based on trust. When you think about it, most of what we do in life—driving in traffic, working, being paid each week for doing our jobs well and correctly, shopping and banking, marriage and family relationships, even getting along with our neighbors—is based on varying degrees of trust. Face it. None of us wants to deal with a person who is not trustworthy. And we certainly would not want to follow a leader who is not trustworthy.

Trust is a key quality of leadership. To be a worthy leader, you have to be trustworthy. Leadership not only starts in our own life but begins primarily at home, where family leadership requires a member to be trustworthy and worthy of being followed. Every parent is in a leadership position. Our children need to know they can trust us, that what we say is true, and that we live our lives on the right path. We need to trust that our boss is running the company ethically and with sound business practices and treating each employee fairly. If we can't trust our leaders in government, our democratic system is in danger.

When you have the quality of trustworthiness, people want

to be like you, to be your friend, to follow you, to be in business with you or partner with you. When you consider the kind of people you want to associate with in any type of relationship, one quality you surely look for is trustworthiness.

I've built all of my relationships on trust. All the buildings at Amway—from the earliest and smallest manufacturing plant to all the other structures in our mile-long complex—we built with just a handshake. The Amway Grand Plaza Hotel was built with a handshake; we never had a contract. Dan Vos, our contractor in the early days, would give us a plan with a cost estimate, and Jay and I would say, "Fine, let's do it." When the work was done, Dan would total his bills and say, "Here's the cost, and here's my 10 percent." He would just take 10 percent of the total as his profit. We started with a little building, so there wasn't a lot at stake. But Dan showed himself trustworthy, and we continued with the same agreement for the big buildings.

Unfortunately, not all people are as trustworthy as Dan. We'll always have to deal with those whose word means nothing and who try to beat the system for their own gain. As a result of mistrust, we've become more leery of strangers. Some banks or stores require at least two pieces of identification to cash a check and have to guard against identity theft, and we are required to remove our shoes before getting through heightened airport security to guard against terrorism. Yet, the bad checks and security threats are actually rarities when you consider how many business transactions are conducted every day. Fortunately, our society and economy continue to operate because most of us agree to be trustworthy.

In my business partnership with Jay, our trust was such that either one of us could make a decision, costing whatever amount, and the other would just accept it. It was implicitly understood that we were both committed to what either one of us decided. Jay would say, "Well, if Rich made the commitment, that's good enough for me." Or I'd say, "Okay, it's all right. Whatever Jay says goes. If he's here alone and I'm not here, then he makes the decisions."

Trust is developed through experience. My trust with Jay was established from the beginning of our friendship. We had been talking about getting into business together since high school. The only question was, "What kind of business?" In fact, I was still serving overseas just after World War II when Jay started our aviation business. He got home earlier than I did after the war and was checking around about starting a flying school because we were convinced aviation was going to be a big thing after World War II. With so many airplanes and pilots in the war, we imagined that everybody was going to have an airplane in his backyard. That never happened, but the aviation industry still became big in ways we could not have dreamed.

I was still in the Marianas Islands when Jay sent me a letter saying he was talking to this guy who was going to build a new airport on the north end of town, in a small community—a neighborhood airport, so to speak. He said the airport owner was looking for investors to help operate the airport, give flying lessons, and offer other flight services. So I told my dad to give Jay all the money I had, what I had managed to save from my monthly Air Force pay of sixty dollars, which was seven hundred dollars. Turning over my life's savings with no questions asked was in essence saying to my friend Jay, "I trust you."

Trust is essential in a friendship, but we also need trust in community. Just think how our whole society works on trust. In a society without trust, businesses would hardly function because contracts would hold no value. Traffic wouldn't move out of mistrust that cars would run red lights. Parents wouldn't allow their children to attend school out of mistrust for the teachers. Our towns and cities would come to a standstill without a basic level of assumed trust.

Businesses, societies, and even our world community require trust to function. When countries fail to cooperate with one another or build relationships, the roadblock often is a lack of trust. Their politicians are dishonest. They are unable to confront each other, look each other in the eye, and commit to a solution.

During the Cold War, the best Ronald Reagan could do when dealing with the Soviet Union was a policy of "trust but verify." We had to verify the Soviets' weapon capabilities because we could not trust what they said at summit meetings or the negotiating table. The wheels come off and the trains cannot really run on time in any organization, society, or relationship without trust—whether it's between marriage partners, within a church, or in a school. If you can't trust a teacher to show up daily or to mark honestly and not give higher grades to favorites, trust breaks down. If we cannot trust those in authority or those who hold great responsibilities—from police officers to the president of the United States—we lose the glue that holds our society together.

Even in a trustworthy society, we can remain skeptical of another person's word because we've been burned by false advertising or broken promises or undependable people. So we've added safeguards, those backup systems that are phrases or gestures to let people know we're true to our word. We make sure we shake on it or we "swear to God and hope to die," if we're not telling the truth, or we place our right hand on a stack of

Bibles or sign contracts. But the Bible tells us to be trustworthy by simply making our yes mean yes and our no mean no—no frills required. Our word alone should be sufficient in a trustworthy society.

With a worldwide business dealing with millions of people, I've simply had to embrace the fact that nearly all people are trustworthy and that I need to put my trust in people. I put my trust in strangers half a world away. We pack a shipping container with Amway products manufactured at our plants in Ada, Michigan, and put the container on a truck or train for delivery to the West Coast, where it's loaded on a ship headed for Tokyo. From there, the shipment is redistributed throughout Asia, or some of the products may be loaded aboard other vessels for Sydney, Australia. Those products are then ordered and sent to our distributors throughout Australia. I would have trouble sleeping if I could not put my trust in people to ensure that all these products are delivered to the right people on time.

Trust means we deliver as promised. I learned early in business that success depends on that simple principle. Our first Amway product, which we named L.O.C. (Liquid Organic Cleaner), was produced for us by a fledgling manufacturer in Detroit. This was the first company we did business with, and the owner proved to be totally unreliable. He couldn't put together a consistent product. He sold us products first with red caps, but a later order would have yellow caps, and the next, blue. Sometimes the liquid was clear and other times yellow. He owed money from past business dealings, so whatever we paid him he used to pay off debts and then had no money to buy the raw materials he needed to make more products.

Sometimes we'd get bottles that he bought from another supplier with labels for a different product beneath our labels. We once received a shipment where our labels fell off— revealing that they had been pasted over bottles made for a toilet bowl cleaner! Because he was so unreliable, we found another supplier who said he could manufacture the same type of product. But the original supplier, saying we had stolen his formula, sued us for a quarter of a million dollars. Jay and I got a good laugh out of the fact that he assumed we—or our little business—were worth that much! We learned a couple of important lessons. We needed people we could trust to make a product with consistent quality and reliable delivery. And we knew that products do not sell themselves and that our business succeeded by building relationships with people and earning their trust. Amway today manufactures hundreds of products. We are stringent about a level of quality control that enables us to sell all of them with a satisfaction guarantee. And all of our products are sold friend to friend, family member to family member. People buy from people they can trust.

Trust is based on the Golden Rule: trusting that people will treat us as they would like to be treated not only is assuring but encourages us to be trustworthy. I am proud that our business plan has never wavered. Year after year, for fifty years, people in the Amway business have been compensated according to the business plan based on the sales of their products and the sales of products by others they sponsor into the business. If someone sponsors a person into the Amway business, that person remains in the sponsor's line of sponsorship. That's trust; that's a responsibility they have. Even after people are dead, we continue to pay their descendants the share of profits generated by their Amway business.

You can appreciate what it means when someone bestows the honor upon you of saying "I trust you." I trust you to complete this job even when I'm not here to look over your shoulder. I trust you with heavy responsibility. I trust you to meet me when you say you will. I trust you to pay back that loan. I trust you with the car keys.

To have the most positive influence when telling someone we trust them, we must protect our own reputation for being trustworthy. Trust can be quickly destroyed when we fail to deliver as promised or go back on our word. Misplaced trust is difficult to recover. This is especially true with children. When you tell your kids you're going to do something for them, make sure you do it. That's what builds their trust. If you can't do what you said, tell them honestly so that you're not misleading them. Even when it hurts, we need to learn to be absolutely truthful with our children.

When I was growing up, my parents would often say, "You know we can't afford that," when I asked for something. That was an easy and truthful answer. An honest answer is important so people can rely on what we say. We need to level with them at all times, whatever our answer. We need to think through our answers about what we can or can't, will or won't do. If you speak to people honestly, you will always have their trust.

One gains trust by being trustworthy, but you likely know people who've proven to be untrustworthy. Perhaps some people with whom you've done business have cheated a bit, haven't provided all the details on an order, or have begun to do sloppy work as soon as they were comfortable they had you as a steady customer. People like these betray your trust. I've sailed a lot in my life, and I would compare the dangers of losing trust in our society with that of losing trust on a sailboat. Sailing is a team sport and can be dangerous. A big sailboat has a lot of moving parts and a lot that can go wrong and hurt people when winds howl and storms blow in.

I recently talked to a young man who has raced with us. He's a bowman, the crew member who must always be ready to go aloft to untangle a line or fix a jammed sail. He faces the prospect of a line snapping that can suddenly send him flying to the top of the mast or falling to the deck. He shared a recent experience in which he started to swing uncontrollably from a line that connected him to the mast high up. The boat was rocking in a storm and lightning was flashing. At the top of the mast he was trying to free a sail that was jammed, when suddenly he flipped over in his harness and was knocked out cold. Each time the boat rocked, he would swing and crash into the mast. By the time the rest of the crew could free him and get him down, he had been really banged around and was unconscious. Sailing at just seven or eight knots, the boat was hours away from a port. They finally got him into a hospital, and he healed. But the point is that sailing, like life, has its dangers, and we need to trust others to help do what we cannot do alone.

You need to trust your crewmates on a sailboat. Lines can snap and things can go flying. A winch can be dangerous if the person running it doesn't act quickly enough. Sailing is definitely a team sport that requires great coordination. As in life, it's not without its dangers, especially when it's rough. Sailing is teamwork, and there must be trust among the helmsman and the captain who's calling changes and the navigator below and the crew in the bow who are constantly pulling and adjusting sails and straightening fouled lines. They must trust each other to do their jobs well, because the slightest mistake can mean anything from a lost finger to a man overboard. Life is teamwork. As in sailing, where there's trust among the captain and the navigator and the whole crew that each is doing his specialized job, so in life. We need to trust those who know more than we do. Life can be dangerous. We need to trust people to do their jobs and not act in ways that are harmful to the rest of us.

On the Orlando Magic team, trust comes down to unselfishness. Each player wants to increase his own records and points scored, but sharing the ball is the key for them to achieve this. The player who doesn't have a clear shot needs to pass, even though he'd really like to take the shot. Besides passing, players also have to be unselfish by doing their job on both ends of the court. Basketball is exhausting, with players constantly running up and down the court and switching quickly between offense and defense. Playing defense is especially exhausting. Players' legs tire and they start missing shots. They lose their rhythm for shooting. Players need that instant response to switch between being a defender and being a shooter. It takes a lot of physical ability and mental discipline to switch from offense to defense and back, but that's what's needed to make a team from a group of individuals. Trust means being unselfish — doing what's best for everyone, even when there may be opportunity to better oneself. We need the discipline to perform all that is required of a team.

"I trust you": Saying this powerful phrase helps cement relationships among people who depend on each other. We need trust as our personal, unwritten contract in our families, marriages, workplaces, and communities. We need to say "I trust you" as our sign of the confidence we hold in people with whom we share a special bond in supporting relationships. Like a sailing crew or a basketball team, our society operates on trust. We depend upon one another like teammates do. Telling someone "I trust you" sends a special message. I still look forward to every opportunity to tell my children and grandchildren or a friend or business associate, "I trust you."

9

"I respect you"

My father, Simon, always had a good reputation. Everybody liked Si. I'm sure he was liked because he liked and respected people back. One of the most valuable lessons he taught me was that each person has value and is gifted in some way. No matter what or who they are or what they do, everyone is important to someone. Therefore, we learn to respect them. You earn respect by showing respect. Using the phrases in this book really comes down to showing respect for everyone we know and meet. Once we begin to look for the positive in everyone and seek out qualities we respect about them, showing respect becomes a habit. While the other phrases in this book are powerful when spoken, respect is a bit more complex. Saying the words "I respect you" is very powerful, but respect really must be earned and demonstrated. Respect is reciprocal. If you want to be respected, you must respect others. People know when you value and respect them and when you don't. It's difficult to hide disrespect, and people can sense your attitude almost instinctively.

I had a friend who would always line up his dollar bills in order of amount and carefully fold his money in his wallet. I finally asked him why he persisted in this meticulous routine. He said, "I respect money, so I treat it with respect." If only earning and showing respect in human relationships was this easy! People automatically respect money, but we all have to work to earn and show respect to people.

It's been said there are two types of people—those who enter a room and say, "Here I am!" and those who come in and say, "Ah, there you are." We need to be the second type. Earning and showing respect begins with listening to people. Everyone has some achievement in his or her life. If you ask someone a few questions and learn a little about that person, you'll discover reasons to say, "I respect you." I'm sometimes asked by people before going to a luncheon or other event, "What should I talk about?" I recommend that they ask questions. Conversation is easy when you just ask questions. People have commented to me that I seem to have great conversations at social gatherings. When I consider my conversations, I realize that I hardly talk at all. I ask a lot of questions. For example, I was once conversing with one of my nieces at a family gathering and started a conversation with some simple questions: "How are your kids doing? Isn't one just getting out of high school?" This was her opening for telling me about how her son graduated third in his high school class of six hundred and had scholarship offers from four major universities. Wow, that achievement I can respect! When her son came up to me later, I knew of his achievement and could say, "Congratulations! I respect you!"

When my son, Dick, ran for governor, he was advised that one thing he needed to learn was the one-minute meet and greet. Candidates need to shake as many hands as possible during a campaign. That requires greeting each person and spending no more than a minute before moving on to the next person. This was not natural for Dick, who was accustomed to talking with people, asking questions, listening, and looking people in the eye. He was taught to respect people, no matter who they were. His natural inclination may not have served him best in a campaign, but I believe he still gained a reputation as a man who respects people because he listens. Respect becomes part of your nature when you show an interest in people and listen. You soon gain a reputation in your community as a respecter of people.

Discovering reasons to respect people is actually easy, because everybody is happy to talk about themselves. You never have a lull in a conversation if you just ask people about their lives. Some people, in fact, never tire of talking about what they think or what they're doing. There's a story about a guy who was going on and on talking about himself. Finally he said, "But that's enough about me. Now, tell me what *you* think of me!" Most of the people we meet are a bit more reticent, but encouraging them to talk about themselves is powerful. Just to be asked about what we do or our opinion is a great compliment. Many times in conversation, people can't wait to cut in to share their experiences or offer their opinions. That's human nature. We want to be respected, loved, and appreciated. If that's the case, then we should seek out virtues and achievements we can respect about an individual. Then we can say, "That's great! I respect you for that!" With so many people trying to get respect, it's important that you and I show respect.

Showing interest in everyone we meet is one of the highest forms of respect. Will Rogers once said, "I never met a man I didn't like." That statement might be difficult to believe for the typical person who may suffer a difficult coworker, not see eye to eye with a next-door neighbor, or simply runs across others who are unlikable. I have an idea that Will Rogers was the type of individual who showed enough interest in everyone he met to discover something he could like about them. There might have been a case or two where I couldn't find much, if anything, to respect about a person, but that likely was because I didn't have ample opportunity to talk to that person.

I truly can say, however, that I've always been fascinated by people and have a genuine love for them. I even invented a little game to help me learn more about people I already know but could get to know better. The game is called "You're in the Box!" When we gather with family or friends, we'll pick one person to be "in the box." If it's your turn, you tell us your life story, and we get to ask questions. I've found that the game works really well onboard a boat when people are relaxed after a day on the water and have nowhere to run if they might be reluctant to talk about themselves! It's amazing to discover how little we really know about each other, often even our best friends. We can learn so much just by listening. I don't learn the life story of everyone I meet, but people often remark to me about how I seem to enjoy stopping to meet a variety of people and learning something about them. I'm enriched by learning even a little about the person who serves me in a restaurant or pulls into the next boat slip or sits next to me in a waiting room.

We need to be interested in people and listen to them, but showing and earning respect also can be as simple as remembering names and faces. When people acknowledge us by name—especially when it's someone important who remembers our name—we feel respected. I respect President George H. W. Bush. When I walked into a room where he was, he would say, "Hi, Rich." He didn't have to say, "I respect you," because in the big, wild world of Washington, D.C., and the thousands of people he meets, he made a point of remembering my name. Learning to call people by their name shows our respect for them. A lot of people don't pay any attention to names, but I think it's essential for building relationships. If I'm going to an event and I don't know people's names, I feel a bit awkward. I'll even review a guest list of people I haven't seen in a while as a reminder of names before attending large events. Getting into the habit of remembering names and faces by itself shows respect. When I'd walk through a plant at Amway and the people would yell, "Hi, Rich," I believe that friendly atmosphere was built on my making it a point to know those employees' names.

When I show respect to the people who are part of my life, what do I get? Respect. Showing respect begins with simply forgetting about ourselves for a moment and being aware of the other person. I've practiced this type of respect for many years at Amway with our employee meetings. We respected the opinions and abilities of our employees because first we respected them as people. We felt they should have an opportunity to speak up around the table with us and offer their perspectives and suggestions. They got to know me, and I got to know them by asking questions and listening. They got to see that I wasn't such a bad guy and wanted to treat them fairly. That's how respect is built. A suggestion box is a wonderful sign of respect. If we ignore people because our heads are too high in the clouds (or our nose is too high in the air), we're making a big mistake. If we really want to be important, we'll pay attention to others and show respect to everyone. That's how to really become important.

True respect knows no social or economic barriers. It must extend to anyone in any walk of life. In the early days of Amway we had an employee who did all of our yard work and snow removal. I once said to him, "Harry, you always do a terrific job. Why don't you put your name in for another job inside the company to advance?" He said, "No, I like the job I have, and I want to just stay out here doing what I'm doing. Don't worry about me; don't try to promote me." He could only have said that because he felt worthy in his job and knew he was respected. I complimented him often on the great job he was doing so that he would know he was respected and appreciated.

I also remember one of our truck drivers whose driving skills we so respected that we promoted him to manage our truck fleet. A year later he said, "Take me out of this job; it's not for me, I want to get behind the wheel again." He had enough self-respect to understand and say what he liked and didn't like. He didn't enjoy supervising people. He enjoyed driving a truck! He felt respected for doing a job that was important to the success of the company. He was comfortable in an environment in which respect was not based on position or title.

When we consider that each person is created in the image of God with a purpose in life, we dignify all people by treating them as we ourselves wish to be treated. God has a job for everybody. Everybody has a role in life. We need to respect everyone rather than compare our talents and occupations with theirs. When we get into the arguments that "we're better than you are" or "I'm stronger than you are," we are showing disrespect. When we categorize or stereotype people, we rob them of their dignity and personality. We demean and dismiss them according to our own prejudices. Living life in comparison with others is futile. We'll always have people ahead of us and behind us. Playing the comparison game might be part of our competitive spirit, but it's a bad and disrespectful game.

True respect should be shown regardless of differences in politics, religion, or background. We can come from different backgrounds or disagree on viewpoints but still respect one another. Our political parties once were much more respectful of each other's views than they are today. Republicans and Democrats used to get together for the greater cause. They could argue about domestic matters but agreed on foreign affairs. Arthur Vandenberg, a Michigan senator from Grand Rapids from 1928 to 1951, was well known for being skilled in getting the two sides to come together in a respectful way to get things done. Tip O'Neill, Speaker of the U.S. House of Representatives from 1977 to 1987, was a master at that, too. He was able to get people who disagreed on an issue to at least respect each other. We can disagree on policies without condemning people personally. When we learn the art of listening and being interested sincerely in other people and their points of view, we can then use the powerful phrase "I respect you." To tell a person you respect him or her is high praise. Those are sweet words.

We also need to show respect for the personal decisions and feelings of others, even when their decisions may be contrary to what we believe is in our best interest. Billy Donovan, head coach of the Florida Gators, signed a contract to be the coach of the Magic just after Florida won the 2007 national NCAA basketball championship. The signing was announced at a news conference and was covered by ESPN and other national sports media. He then changed his mind and decided he wanted to remain in Gainesville and continue to coach college ball rather than go to the NBA. He called me to explain, and after listening to him, I told him that although I didn't agree with him I respected his wishes and released him from his contract. A few weeks later he called me out of the blue to thank us for the classy way in which management handled the situation. That's just an illustration of how we need to maintain respect always and in all ways.

As with trust, respect is at the heart of all successful relationships from marriage and family to business and sports. I talk to my Orlando Magic players and encourage them to respect each other. A team sport must be built around respect for the game and for your fellow player. Great coaches know how to encourage their players and earn their respect. In basketball, although each player wants to score the points and make a name for himself, he is also given credit for assists, in recognition of and respect for the talents and contributions of each player. Teamwork is not possible without respect and trust. That's true in sports and in business. My partnership with Jay survived only because we had mutual respect. When Jay or I were on the road, we never worried about what was going on back at the company because each of us, in the absence of the other, could make a decision for both. That's respect.

The foundation for respect begins in the home. We learn to have respect for our parents and sisters and brothers. A family's goal is to uphold everybody in both the immediate and the extended family, and to wish the best for everyone. When you hear about cousins or nephews doing well, you congratulate them. You uphold each other and show concern about the well-being of each member. When you do that, and do it well, a family is truly born.

We decided to keep our business family-owned. That also takes respect. Our son Doug is in charge now and the rest of the family respects him and has confidence in him to make good decisions. We now are responsible for ensuring that our third generation understands the family business and that our family is responsible for millions of employees and independent business owners whom they need to respect and appreciate. Jay and I started with the conviction that many people in America wanted to have a business of their own. We have since found that many people worldwide want to have a business of their own! Our conviction was based on respect for people. Had we not been convinced that people were worthy and could be trusted and respected, we could not have started a business.

I'm gratified that so many of our employees feel they are respected as though they are part of a family. Nick Anderson was a member of the Magic when our family bought the team. He told me about a year ago that playing for the Magic was the only job he ever really loved, and that he wanted to get back with the Magic in any capacity that might be available. "Being a part of the Magic was my life. That was my family," he told me. Nick has talents as a people person and is now a goodwill ambassador for the Magic in a variety of ways that support the organization. I'm glad to know that he wanted to come back because the Magic was like family. As a family business, we want people to know they are respected.

A business, relationship, or any organization without respect for its members is doomed to failure. An organization that changes from one in which members work together with respect to one of self-interest and internal squabbles is on a downward spiral. I've noticed over the years a typical pattern in organizations that evolve from an atmosphere of respect to self-interest. These organizations typically go through four stages: (1) the creating stage; (2) the managing stage; (3) the defending stage; (4) the blaming stage. In the first stage, someone has a vision or dream to build. Others respect that person's dream and enthusiastically join the excitement of building something new. In the second stage, people start to divert time and energy from building and creating to focusing on organizing and managing what has been created. Stage three is an era of fighting to stay ahead of the competition and being concerned with preserving what has been built. The fourth stage is when an organization turns inward and members begin squabbling with each other, competing with each other to get ahead, and blaming each other for any setbacks. The excitement of building and creating has been forgotten. It's time to divide the spoils. Perhaps you've noticed this pattern in your workplace, school, church, or government. I believe we need more positive leaders who can show and earn respect in order to redirect many of our institutions to the excitement and productivity of the creating stage.

Not all organizations or people are going to be respectful of others. We'll have times when we feel respected and times when we're disrespected. I learned this early in my life and discovered that along with earning and showing respect, we need to learn how to remain positive in the face of disrespect. I can still remember one of the first times I felt what it meant to be respected by a crowd. My "Selling America" speech was the beginning for me of feeling that I and my views on something about which I felt strongly had earned the respect of my listeners—not just for building a business but for my public stand on how I felt about this wonderful country. That was my

first public forum, and I recall wondering if my talk was suffi-
ciently worthy to gain the respect of our local newspaper and be
recognized in it. I'm happy to say it was, and that was important
to me! We can all get our names in the paper at least twice—
when we're born and when we die. But I believe we'd all like to
see our names in the paper a few more times as a sign of respect
for something we said or achieved.

As I became more involved in our community and as my
reputation grew as a business founder, my name was frequently
in my hometown newspaper. I also got to know the newspaper
editor, whom I told one day, "You know, that story about Amway
you printed on the front page was not a front-page story." "No,"
he said, "the story is not, but you are. Stories related to you are
front-page news because of your involvement in the community." For better or worse, that's the ultimate in respect.

I now find it interesting and a bit amusing that one of my
first encounters with newspapers was one of disrespect. In the
early days of Nutrilite we tried to advertise for distributors in
the classified sections of newspapers. The advertisement simply
read: "Make $1,000 a month part time. Complete training avail-
able." A lot of papers wouldn't run our ad because we couldn't
guarantee the claim. I responded that I couldn't guarantee the
income but at least the opportunity was there for anyone who

wanted to work. A lot of people were disrespectful to Jay and me and our Amway business. They ridiculed us and said that our business would never work. We learned to just ignore people like that. If you believe in what you're doing, you have to move forward against the disrespectful crowd. As Jay liked to say, "The dogs may bark, but the caravan moves on."

Some people show disrespect because they have a negative view of people. A banker I knew once told me that our Amway business would never work because people could not be trusted. In our business, distributors were responsible for passing on monthly bonuses to others in their group. The banker asked me, "What makes you think everybody will pay those bonuses?" I said, "Because people are basically honest." It had never occurred to me that people might not pay bonuses! Our company ensured the payment of all bonuses, and very rarely did we have an instance of a distributor's failing to pay one. That shows the power of respect and trust — positive powers that can overcome the doubts of disrespectful, negative people.

I've learned that a powerful way to overcome disrespect is simply to show respect. Many years ago when I arrived in Australia as part of the America's Cup challenger trials, the Australians treated the American team with hostility. The New York Yacht Club had been vilified over the years for their furious defense of the cup, so the Australians viewed Americans as "those Yanks" who would do anything to win. The NYYC had held the America's Cup for 132 years but lost it that year (1983) to the Australians, who were very proud of being the first country to win the cup from the United States. Many Australians used the occasion to jeer at the Americans, and even some of the customs agents taunted them when they were leaving because they had lost the cup. But when my group and I first went to Australia, I'd made a point of being friendly and gracious, shaking hands and chatting with the Australian people. Eventually, we fell short in our bid and were eliminated from the trials, but I believe we did our part to leave the Australian people with a better impression of our team and country, and they saw these "Yanks" weren't so bad after all.

Another counterpoint to respect that we need to work to overcome is rejection. Sooner or later in life, we all need to deal with rejection. I felt the ultimate rejection when I needed a new heart to save my life and was rejected by every heart center in the United States. They all said that at the age of seventy I was too old to benefit from a transplant. Finally one surgeon in the U.K. accepted me. That's how it is in life. We can be rejected by many, and then the Lord opens the door to that one person who turns the tide. In our Nutrilite business, we knew that on average if we called on four people, one of them would buy. In sales as in life, you often need to overcome much rejection before you succeed in earning respect. But if you believe in yourself and others you can overcome rejection and earn respect by showing respect.

Because of my long experience in sales or perhaps just my nature, I'm not overly concerned with rejection or people who are not respectful. My focus always has been on the one person in four who says, "Yes." Friends who remember me from high school tell me, "Oh, man, you were always positive; you were always leading the parade; you were always the chief fun maker." I don't remember if I was or not, but obviously some people remember me as that spirited person. I believe that was undoubtedly because my parents created a household built around love and respect. When you feel respected in your home, you're joyful. If you don't feel respected, it's very hard for you to express respect to others. You can't be positive and confident if you're not feeling respected. I would recommend to anyone that he or she work on earning respect through good character, because that's vital to a successful future, and we all have that power within our grasp. Ask questions, listen, and show sincere interest when you meet someone for the first time. Show respect in your demeanor as well and you'll begin to feel good about yourself as well as the other person.

As I consider my years in leadership roles, I'm convinced that respect for others is a most essential trait for leaders. A basic knowledge of business and how to run an organization is of limited value if you cannot respect the people with whom you work and those whom you serve. If they cannot respect you, then you are not a leader. I've known people in positions of leadership who try to demand respect by throwing their weight around or trying to motivate by fear rather than encouragement. Respect doesn't arrive on demand! You all have leaders in your work and life. If you think about the ones you respect, I'm willing to bet they're the ones who earned your respect by showing an interest in you. The big boss you respect and admire the most is likely the one who remembers your name, comments on the good job you're doing, or stops to chat and ask about your family. Earning respect is simple. It doesn't take sophisticated skills or a degree in management but it's essential to successful leadership. As leaders in their homes, parents need to earn and show respect with their children by listening to them and dealing with them fairly. Teachers, as leaders in their classrooms, can show respect by being aware of each of their students' individual circumstances and needs. Doctors earn and show respect by getting to know more about their patients than what is written on their charts. Leaders in any number of careers have opportunities to earn respect by showing respect.

We all want and need to be respected. If you want respect, I recommend you show respect by taking an interest in other people. Ask a few questions. Listen to people who are eager to share with you the proud moments of their lives. You'll quickly discover something about them for which you can say, "I respect you." In so doing, you also will earn their respect, and as a respected person, you will gain self-respect.

10

"I love you"

To say "I love you" and mean it with all your heart has remarkable power. When I think about how my wife, Helen, has enhanced and complemented my life, it's easy to believe that God put us together. Our love kept growing over the years, eventually spreading to include four children, their spouses, and sixteen grandchildren.

Thank God Helen and I expressed those feelings to each other many years ago. After more than fifty years of marriage, we can remember meeting each other in vivid detail. I was riding down a Grand Rapids street with a friend. We noticed two attractive girls (one of which was Helen) walking whom my friend knew and offered to give them a ride home. We dropped Helen off at her home first. As she was leaving the car, I asked the friend her name. She wrote Helen's name and phone number in my school psychology book. I still have that book with her name and phone number written on the inside cover.

I called Helen for our first date, and on a beautiful Sunday afternoon I took her flying. A short time later Helen and a friend's two little girls were enjoying a stroll down some docks near where Helen was visiting for a few days with the girls and their mother. They walked right past where *Salud,* a boat Jay and I owned, was tied up—and I was on it. I offered the three of them a ride—I was just going to gas up the boat at the next dock, but the little girls were thrilled and Helen consented. So after offering her rides in a car, plane, and boat, I continued to call her for dates. Before too long, we were engaged, and a year later, on February 7, 1953, we were married.

Helen later told me that when we first met she thought I was pretty cocky. In fact, my own mother warned her, "You have to stand up to Rich, because those DeVoses will push you around." But Helen said she discovered that what she once thought of as cockiness was really self-assurance and what she at first called "a gift of gab" was actually the gift of connecting, of communication. So when we love each other, we learn to appreciate each other's talents.

Helen has always been positive, supportive, and encouraging. She has guided our marriage and our family and even our business with her foundation of spiritual faith. She has kept us focused on our values and what is truly important in life. She also has been very generous in giving to others because she feels it's incumbent on people to share and that sharing is being obedient to God. So, many of our philanthropic projects have stemmed from Helen's faith. Helen also is a great friend. She lives by the motto, "To have a friend, you have to be a friend." Because of her, our home, outings on boats, and travels always have been filled with friends—friends whom we enjoy and who enjoy each other.

"I love you" is the powerful phrase that encompasses all the others. The way we feel about people—whether it's romantic love, family relationships, or even close friendships—is a form of love. We have to love one another; that's the biblical admonition as expressed by Jesus Christ. Love is a warmer way to express ourselves than saying, "I respect you" or "I believe in you." It's a more tender way of expressing our feelings for people we admire and appreciate. Love is a term of great trust and belief—the strongest term you can use to speak to another person if you feel that way about them. Saying "I love you" is quite a step for most people.

But there are other kinds of love than the love between a husband and wife. We need to find ways to express our love to others with whom we have close relationships or who play important roles in our lives.

I was encouraged years ago by a close friend of mine to express love more freely to others. Billy Zeoli, the founder of Gospel Films and a friend for many years, is very demonstrative in expressing how he feels about people. Maybe it's part of his Italian heritage, but Billy has never been shy about walking up to people and giving them a big hug. Billy encouraged me to greet people with a hug. Gradually it seemed our whole town was hugging each other—some embracing the custom and others less willing to leave their comfort zone. But hugging is a simple way to say "I love you" without summoning the courage to say the words.

The next step for me was to actually use the words, so I just started saying, "Love ya." That's something you hear among families or between close friends. I listen to our kids in conversations or talking on the telephone, and I always hear "Love ya." It's just two little words, but a reminder to those with whom we're talking that they're loved.

Then I began signing my notes and letters "Love ya" to express a feeling stronger than "sincerely." I don't really know what sincerely is supposed to mean, but "Love ya" sends a definite message. It's become my trademark now. It's a personal relationship, a personal bond. It conveys that we have a special relationship—one in which we can make a deal without putting it in writing; when I tell you I'll be there, I'll be there; you can trust that I'll deliver as promised. It says all those things.

We have to learn to think about how we really feel about other people, be willing to express those feelings and begin to say "I love you." Love exists, not just within a husband-and-wife relationship or guy-and-girl romance. There are different types of love that we need to express.

After Jay died, I found a large box of letters he'd written to me while we were both overseas during World War II. After re-reading many of them, I gave all the letters to his son David, thinking he might like to have them and telling him that they might give him a better insight into our relationship and how it survived for a lifetime. David told me later that he was very touched by the letters. He said they gave him a whole new understanding of the relationship between his father and me and how warmly his father felt toward me.

I remember in one of our many conversations Jay talked about different kinds of love—romantic love, the love between parents and children, the love between siblings, and a love that can develop within the bonds of close friendships. Jay was expressing in his letters to me a form of love, an admiration for the qualities he saw in me that had made him want to be my friend. In his letters to his "Dearest and best buddy," Jay was expressing love for a close friend from whom he was separated at the time by thousands of miles in time of war. When Jay and I were exchanging letters, we were both barely out of high school and far from home. We both needed to know that we had a close friend somewhere in the world and that one day we'd be home again, planning to go into business together and probably dreaming that we'd be a big success. Those letters cemented my trust in him. So when we went into business together, it was just a logical extension of a very strong friendship.

Many years later I wrote in a birthday note to Jay, "Over the past twenty-five-plus years we have had our differences, but something greater has always shown through. I don't know if there is any simple way to say it, but it could be called mutual respect. A better word could be 'love.' " One reason our friendship allowed us to become business partners was that we complemented each other. While Jay would be content to stay home and read a book, he also didn't want to be left out of anything if I told him I was going out. It didn't take a lot of prodding to get him to come along with me. So I think I was an influence in helping Jay be more adventurous. I think he enjoyed me because I brought a little action into his life.

By the same token, I admired Jay greatly. He was an intellectual. He had a lot of wisdom. He knew a lot of things I didn't. He was an excellent student. He read a lot more than I did. So we fed off each other. Our mutual admiration resulted in a love that develops within the bond of a close friendship.

"I love you" also is an especially powerful phrase when said to children. Those words make them feel protected, cared about, believed in; that the person saying these words is really special. So why not say it? If love is something you feel, then saying "I love you" is a manifestation of that feeling. Unfortunately, some people never say "I love you" to their children or anyone else. And often it's because they can't bring themselves to say what they feel, or perhaps they don't take the time or make the effort. With any of these powerful phrases, we must avoid the tendency to leave them unsaid. Most likely there are all sorts of times that we think, "Oh, he's really a great guy, isn't he?" But we don't think about telling him so. We go home from a concert and say, "That was really terrific." Yet we never think about writing a note to express our enjoyment. We need to put our feelings in writing or pass them on personally. We need to make the expression of our feelings a personal habit.

The most important place to express love is with our own families. Deuteronomy 11:1, 19 (NIV) reads: "Love the Lord your God and keep his requirements, his decrees, his laws and his commands always. . . . Teach them to your children, talking about them when you sit at home and when you walk along the road, when you lie down and when you get up." We need to teach our children God's love and express our love to our spouse and children. When I attend a graduation ceremony or see children leave home to start their own lives, my prayer is that their parents have taught their children well and instilled in them the values that will carry them successfully through life. I hope they can build their lives from a firm foundation of a loving family.

I have very warm memories of my childhood and growing up in a close-knit family. We faced some tough times and financial struggles, but we met those challenges together. We often lacked for money, but we never lacked for love. Looking back, sharing a home as an extended family with my grandparents during the Depression was actually a blessing that brought us closer together and exposed me to the wisdom and role models of two generations.

Family is the foundation of our faith and values. My parents and grandparents instilled in me a faith in Jesus Christ that has remained at the center of my life. My family shaped within me a love of country and freedom. My home was the incubator of the American dream. I was fortunate to have parents who raised me to believe in myself enough to seize the limitless opportunities our country offers. Teach your grandchildren the fundamental lessons of life. Talk to them about right and wrong and the values you hold to in life. Be a role model. Give them the gift of your life experience. Building a firm foundation of family takes work but pays dividends by ensuring each generation is instilled with the faith and values that are at the heart of abundant lives and a moral society.

I was a happy child despite few material possessions. I continue to be a happy person today. But my wealth has not made me any happier than when I was a kid growing up during the Depression. The love of my family keeps me happy. I treasure the company of my wife after more than fifty years of marriage. I'm proud of each of our four children and their spouses and how they have created their own loving families. And Helen and I are enjoying watching our grandchildren grow and are looking forward to seeing them mature and make their own way in the world. We pray for them all every day — by name.

While we all know the intimate love of marriage and family, I hope we also all can appreciate a form of love that I believe exists beyond family and even close friends. Love comes in all forms. You can love someone in a very personal way. You can love your children in a slightly different way. You can love your doctor for what he does for you. I love my cardiologist, Rick McNamara. I can tell him that easily. He's terrific and he cares about me; therefore, I love him. We can love our friends. As I told you, our family's phrase is always "Love ya." But now I have friends who, by my example, say that to me. A friend who is a businessman in a little town in Tennessee always ends our phone conversations with "Love ya." So we can have relationships between friends based on a different kind of a love — one involving respect and admiration. We need to consider love in many ways and on different terms between different people.

We can even have love for a time or place that were special in our lives. Many of us have a strong allegiance to our high schools or colleges even decades after graduation. I can truly say that I still love my high school and am grateful for the teachers and the loving, encouraging atmosphere that had an impact on my life. Helen and I provided the lead gift to build the Center for Arts and Worship at my old school, Grand Rapids Christian High. Students at Christian High had no place where they all could congregate for chapel services, plays, and other performances. The school has remarkable theater and music programs, but performance areas were ill equipped, cramped, and outdated. As a result of our contribution and the remarkable generosity of our community, these students now enjoy a beautiful auditorium, as well as dressing rooms and rehearsal halls. They now are truly inspired to perform to the best of their abilities. The level of this new facility recognizes the level of their talents. Their families and the community enjoy an experience enhanced by the auditorium.

For me, it was special to know I could present such a gift to the high school that once had done so much for me. In the lobby, they placed a replica of Jay's Model A, the car in which he gave me rides to school and in which we dreamed about one day going into business together. I can never truly repay that high school or the influence of its people, but I was richly blessed and encouraged that the tradition of my high school continues and that future business and community leaders will get their start at my school.

I also believe in loving communities and know I've been blessed to live in one. I was asked in early 2007 to write the narrative for a coffee-table book titled *West Michigan Visions.* These types of books are published about communities across the United States and are filled with photo essays picturing natural splendors, recreation, commerce, and arts. In my narrative, I included many of the reasons I love West Michigan, including its waters for boating, friendly small towns, and entrepreneurs who provide our quality of life and livelihoods. You could say these types of books exhibit community pride, but I believe they convey a feeling closer to love.

When downtown Grand Rapids was struggling to survive in the 1970s because people and businesses were moving to the suburbs, there was discussion about building a hotel outside Grand Rapids. But Jay and I decided that Amway would remodel a hotel in downtown Grand Rapids because this was our town; we loved it, it was close to our hearts. That decision was the beginning of a rebirth of downtown Grand Rapids that is still continuing. People to this day approach me to say thank you for investing in our community when we could have gone elsewhere. While we do have a lot of interests elsewhere, our foundation's primary giving is in Grand Rapids. From a corporate investment standpoint, we have always built and expanded in our town. We once considered building a major distribution center outside Michigan. We conducted a national survey that showed tax and other advantages to locating in a southern state. Yet, we elected to stay where we were just because it was our home.

When I reflect on that decision and other projects in Grand Rapids, I have a wonderful, warm feeling about having the opportunity to help make our town a better place. There's a big world out there with a lot going on both positive and negative.

But our job is to make our own place better. Home is where we can help instill positive attitudes, create jobs, help our neighbors, and rally our friends to cooperate in partnerships that build a better community. Economics drives much of the progress in our communities, but I believe another motivating factor is the love we feel for hometowns. Love of community is why more people choose to stay where they grew up rather than move away. Love of community is one reason we want to ensure our children have the best schools and our citizens have quality medical care. We love our community for the friendships we've made, the church where we were married, the restaurant in which we celebrate family milestones, or the feeling we get when we walk down our street. We've been commanded to love our neighbors as ourselves. That's the kind of neighborhood where we all would love to live.

I love the businesses I've built and own. I love the Amway business that Jay and I built from the tiny office and warehouse in our basements, which today provides income and hope to people around the world. Amway is still a family business. The Orlando Magic is a family business. Members of our family still oversee the daily operations because we love our businesses and love our work. I've always loved my work, so I feel as if I've never worked a day in my life. I never resented going to work, because it never seemed like work. Work for me was always a good experience, even on the tough days.

I also believe we must show more love for our country. Helen and I provided a major gift to provide for the exhibit hall in the National Constitution Center, which opened July 4, 2003, in Philadelphia as the first museum dedicated to honoring and explaining the U.S. Constitution. We wanted young people today and future generations to appreciate the framework of our free society and the framers who risked their lives to sign their work. I served in the U.S. Army Air Corps during World War II when thousands of young Americans sacrificed their lives for the freedoms we enjoy. We came home convinced that Americans could achieve any goal they set. I spoke up for American democracy and our free enterprise system when half the world's people were denied freedoms in communist and social-ist countries. We named our business after the American Way because we were convinced our economic system was the best in the world and that people wanted the freedom to run their own businesses. I do not deny that our country has problems or claim it has a history without blemish, but I make no apologies for my unabashed love for my country. I grew up in an America in which immigrants were proud of their newly earned U.S. citizenship, citizens were not embarrassed to salute the flag or sing our National Anthem, and we respected the office of U.S. president even if we did not agree with the man and all his policies or were not a member of his political party. If we truly want a positive society of positive people, we need to find love in our hearts for our fellow Americans and our homeland and its democratic principles and "can do" philosophy that have given us the blessings of liberty and the economic advantages we enjoy.

So, love is all around us. We need to look for and nurture love—for our God who blesses us richly, for marriages, for families, for friends, and for our communities. Let's not just think about saying "I love you" and regret later that we didn't say it. Let's take every opportunity to tell our loved ones—from our hearts—"I love you." Or maybe just say "Love ya" to someone you admire or appreciate. If you can't say the words, at least give someone a hug. And make it a big one!

Jesus said the greatest commandment is to love the Lord our God with all our hearts and the second is to love our neighbors as ourselves. Let's all use our hearts. Say "I love you." With this and all the other powerful phrases, we can all make our homes, communities, and world more positive places to live.